The 50s Compass

Finding Your True North in Midlife

SARAH ONG

First published by Ultimate World Publishing 2025
Copyright © 2025 Sarah Ong

ISBN

Paperback: 978-1-923425-65-1
Ebook: 978-1-923425-66-8

Sarah Ong has asserted her rights under the Copyright, Designs and Patents Act 1988 to be identified as the author of this work. The information in this book is based on the author's experiences and opinions. The publisher specifically disclaims responsibility for any adverse consequences which may result from use of the information contained herein. Permission to use information has been sought by the author. Any breaches will be rectified in further editions of the book.

All rights reserved. No part of this publication may be reproduced, stored in or introduced into a retrieval system, or transmitted in any form, or by any means (electronic, mechanical, photocopying, recording or otherwise) without the prior written permission of the author. Any person who does any unauthorised act in relation to this publication may be liable to criminal prosecution and civil claims for damages. Enquiries should be made through the publisher.

Cover design: Ultimate World Publishing
Layout and typesetting: Ultimate World Publishing
Editor: James Salmon

Ultimate World Publishing
Diamond Creek,
Victoria Australia 3089
www.writeabook.com.au

Dedication

For the women who have entered my life, walked beside me, held me, challenged me and shown me what strength, determination and resilience wrapped in softness looks like.

And for the younger generation growing into women, whose curiosity, courage and passion for life reminds me why it matters to keep showing up and living as an example for you.

You have all brought deep meaning into my life and this book is a quiet thank you; a compass drawn from our shared journey. You all continue to inspire me and I hope to likewise inspire you.

With love,

Sarah xx

Contents

Dedication	1
Preface: Hello and Welcome	5
Introduction	7
Chapter 1: Rediscovering Yourself: Defining Your WHY and Your passion	15
Chapter 2: Thriving in Your 50s: Physical, Emotional and Spiritual Vitality	31
Chapter 3: Guiding with Grace: Parenting Young Adult Children and Nurturing Grandchildren	57
Chapter 4: Redefining Career and Purpose in Your 50s: The Pathway to Retirement	71
Chapter 5: Reflecting on Relationships and Connections: Who Are Your People?	83
Chapter 6: The Exciting Road Ahead: Setting Intentions for an Inspiring and Fulfilling Next Chapter	99
Afterword: Writing the Next Chapter with Intention	111
Epilogue	115
About the Author	119
Special Thanks	121
Words into Actions	125
Speaker Bio	127
Disclaimer	129

Preface

Hello and Welcome

If you're holding this book in your hands, chances are you're searching for something – a spark, a shift, a moment to put yourself first. Maybe life has nudged you in a new direction – a change in relationships, a career transition, an empty nest, or a deeper longing for something *more*. And now, you find yourself at a crossroads, asking: What's next for me?

There may be other questions that are swimming about in your thoughts;

Is it too late to start something new or to even start over?
What does vitality look like now for me and how do I maintain it?

The 50s Compass

How do I let go of what is draining me and no longer serving me?
How do I navigate the emotional and physical changes in my life?
What do I do with this newfound energy and direction?

I had all of these questions bubbling up and that's what drove me to write this book. I suddenly realised I was at a time in my life whereby I either took action or continued to ponder the same old questions above. I'm no different to any other person in my life. As I share my thoughts, I hope that the messages and gentle ideas in this book will benefit you in some way.

I wrote this book for women just like you – women in their midlife who are ready to rediscover what truly lights them up. This is your time to embrace energy, joy and purpose as you step into the next chapter of your life. Whether it's redefining balance, reigniting your passions, or simply giving yourself permission to dream again, this journey is yours to create.

There's no magic potion, but there *is* a magical transformation waiting for you – one that starts with small steps, bold choices and a commitment to yourself.

Are you ready to step into the life you *deserve*?

Let's begin.

Introduction

Happiness isn't just an emotion that passes through us; it's a culmination of events, experiences, feelings, choices and perspectives that form our daily lives. As we approach midlife, we can no longer wait for the joy to find us. It's something that we can and must cultivate with intent and purpose. This book is about discovering what truly lights you up, whether it's the smell of the salt air, the satisfaction of finishing a book, the laughter of a grandchild or the quiet gratitude of your life as a whole. By honing in and focussing on the nearby aspects of your life that bring you happiness, you can create the next life chapter that feels fulfilling, meaningful and energising. Let's explore what truly makes your soul sing and how to create an exceptional midlife and beyond.

I never in my wildest dreams thought that I would ever turn fifty. That happened to other people. It happened to my parents, my neighbour, my friend's aunty and my colleague at work... not me! But alas, it did happen! It was actually a pivotal time because I think it gave me permission to stop and recalibrate my life. It gave me the catalyst to say to myself, *'I actually have the tools now to build a future that I am excited to live'*. I can honestly say that I am happy and content with the life I have and my intention for writing this book is to share my story with others who are on the same journey – navigating life in their 50s and defining their true north.

It was a love story that was going to shape the way I would lead my life after turning 50. Yet, when I met him at the age of 20, I had no idea he would have such a profound effect on my life and the way I chose to live it.

It was a Thursday night, the music was creating a party vibe and I moved amongst the crowd happily jigging about and smiling my usual smiley smile. I was all of 20 years of age and really, as a young student nurse, still living at home, going out midweek with my friends and driving my red Ford Laser car, the only thing missing in my life was a cute guy! Enter – Richard. He was of olive complexion, medium height, sporty stature and the cheekiest smile and laugh you could imagine. It was these attributes that drew me directly towards him and before the night drew to a close, I had etched my phone number [560 1573] onto his arm with a biro pen I took from the bar staff. A few days passed and to my surprise and yes, satisfaction, Richard called me from a public pay phone to see what I was doing...

Two years passed and Richard and I were inseparable. We had forged a unique connection. To this day, he is definitely the 'boy' version of me. He drove a sporty little Nissan Coupe and we would cruise around the Mornington Peninsula looking for new fishing spots, particularly around Rye and Flinders. He would take me out onto the pier under a full moon and I'd patiently wait for the squid to bite. He was a master at anything to do with fishing, boats and the ocean. In the winter, we would take to the ski fields. He was so quick at putting the chains on the car, manoeuvring the windy icy

Introduction

roads, carrying the skis and leading the way down the myriad of runs at Mt Buller. I felt totally energised, safe and complete with him.

His personality was also unique. He was adventurous but always in a calculated manner. He took me on what I thought were reckless, bold and sometimes down right ridiculous adventures, but I came to realise that he never took uncalculated risks. Our boating adventures were always done with impeccable preparation of the boat, analysis of the conditions and never would anything be left to chance. He was a scuba diver and windsurfer. All of these sports required deep knowledge, analysis of the situation and ultimately the following of a process.

After my 21st birthday, Richard and I broke up. We parted ways and continued to live the lives that we carved for ourselves. I graduated and became a registered nurse, I travelled throughout Africa, Europe and lived in London for a year with my younger sister. I returned home, undertook further nursing studies, got married, had four children, undertook further Masters studies and began to live what some would describe as the typical suburban lifestyle. Unbeknown to me, Richard followed a similar route but managed to brighten his life with two divorces, selling houses and moving twice, changing jobs and raising as best he could, two beautiful children.

Fast forward a few decades and at the age of 45, whilst having a heated argument with my mother, our fiery exchange was somewhat extinguished when my phone buzzed with a Facebook message alert – Richard. I can vividly remember my thought response to this event: 'What the hell does Richard want?'

As cliché as it sounds, I do believe people come into our lives for a reason. It may be to show us other ways of doing things, expose us to new situations, languages, ways of knowing; the reasons are endless. Suffice to say, Richard and I were reunited again both as adults who had separately led a large part of our lives without any contact whatsoever.

The 50s Compass

We both found ourselves continuing to navigate the similar roads of working in our respective careers, enjoying our independence, nurturing our ageing parents and also raising our teenage children. We both continued to be synergised by our love for the ocean, our sense of adventure and our strong commitment to ensuring that our children were brought up appreciating the education and love we provided that would set them up for their adult lives.

Richard's house looked out over a boat ramp. There was bushland surrounding it and I would love walking down to the ramp, especially at low tide as all the mangroves were exposed and the birdlife was insatiable. At high tide, I would love to sit on the boat ramp with my feet dangling in the water as I contemplated life, often soaking up this reconnection that had occurred between us.

During this time, we continued in our playful ways that banded us together as teenagers. I was just taking up kiteboarding and was having real difficulty riding the board on the water whilst trying to fly a 10-foot kite above me. Who knows what I was thinking? In true Richard style, he took me out on the boat, launching from Sorrento pier and scooting across Port Philip Bay right into the middle where we moored at Mud Island. He helped me take my kiteboarding gear from the boat to the beach and then proceeded to literally sit in the long grasses, shielding himself from the wind and flying sand. He didn't help me set up, run my lines, inflate my kite – nothing. Once kitted up, I looked at him in frustration at his lack of 'helpfulness'. He merely signalled, get out there and practice. It was a sight to be seen, a small lady like me, wrangling a 10-foot kite held up by 20-metre lines in the gusty winds in the middle of Port Philip Bay on a secluded Mud Island. I did manage to ride my board, whilst steering this kite quite a fair way out. I even managed to direct myself back into the beach downwind, which was something that had been holding me back from progressing. I improved so much in this short session but was still frustrated at the lack of support I was getting from Richard. I packed up my

Introduction

gear, which is quite an ordeal, ensuring that I remained vigilant in the wind so that I wasn't taken high into the sky unexpectedly. I was shouting profanities at Richard, expressing my disgust that he merely sat and watched me struggle with this finicky and somewhat dangerous sport. This bout of exuberant profanities was actually being fuelled by the intense sense of accomplishment that ran through my veins after my kiteboarding session.

There was another time when I complained to Richard that I couldn't balance on my surfboard because I wasn't used to positioning my feet sideways on the board. I was used to snow skiing whereby my feet would be facing forward. Another practical lesson was about to ensue. We took the boat out, this time into the middle of Westernport Bay. Richard meticulously set up the tow rope to be let out at the back of the boat and then instructed me to jump in and hold on whilst I had my board secured to my feet. He was such a capable boatsman and gently increased the throttle until I felt the tension in the tow rope and I had no choice but to gather my courage and rise out of the water on my board. I'd never done this before and my first inclination was to bend my arms which saw me faceplant harshly into the water. Richard carefully manoeuvred the boat around and the tow rope was again within arm's reach. Again, I went through the process of holding on, this time being pulled up and I was able to maintain my balance for a tiny second more, before faceplanting once again. I soon grew tired and frustrated at this and called loudly for Richard to let me back onto the boat. Again, in true Richard style, I was signalled to stay in the water and he said I was going to do this eight more times, whether I liked it or not, and only then was I 'allowed' back onto the boat. You could imagine the scenario of yet again, this small lady trying to accomplish a brazen task in the middle of Westernport Bay. Consequently, I did do this eight more times, and each time I got better and better. By the end, I was so ecstatic at my achievements, that I couldn't contain my excitement and pride.

The 50s Compass

Our relationship was so dynamic. I also recall beautiful tender moments where I would lie across his chest as we watched movies like My Octopus Teacher. I particularly loved lying along side him as he strummed his guitar and he practiced the chord combination until it flowed with resonance. He comforted me throughout my most tumultuous times and would hold me in his arms while I cried and cried, and cried some more. He actually taught me that I was strong, determined, powerful and successful, yet I was also vulnerable and highly emotional. He taught me to focus on my passions, practice until I got better and not to rely on anyone to do it for me – for I held all the capabilities myself.

Richard left this world not long after *his* 50th birthday. I'll never forget the words ringing in my ears. The dreaded and feared word beginning with the big 'C'. He deteriorated so quickly. It swept through him like one of those enormous waves we see big wave riders ride at Pipeline or Nazare. One minute they are on the crest of this enormous body of water, then as it begins to barrel, it sweeps and engulfs anything in its path. The surfer is left with nothing but to be floating limp in the intrepid white wash. He has left me heartbroken but with a gift of so many life long lessons, values, beliefs and most of all invaluable memories. These are catalysts that I will take as I continue to navigate my 50s and determine my true north.

Chapter 1

Rediscovering Yourself: Defining Your WHY and Your passion

It's 5.30am and I don't even need the alarm to go off. I'm already awake, eyes wide open and I'm out of bed and heading to the shower. A quick rinse, application of some body oil so my wetsuit is easy to put on, dressed, coffee in hand and I'm heading into the darkness on a two-hour trip towards the Great Ocean Road. All I can think about is, 'What will the waves be like at Urquhart's this morning?' As I drive, I don't have any music on and I love the solidarity that comes with being in my car with my surfboard on the roof. I feel like I am travelling with my soulmate and there doesn't need to be any words spoken.

The 50s Compass

I arrive at the beautiful Urquart's Bluff just as the sun has risen and the day is beginning. There's a group of open water swimmers coming in from their dawn swim. Without sounding ageist, I look at them and say to myself, 'This lot are surely well into their 70s and 80s!' I note this, because I am so interested in what people are doing at the latter stage of their lives. This group of 'older' people, were coming out of the ocean at 7.30am and all I could witness were smiles, laughter and jovial conversations while they walked together up the beach. What an uplifting and inspiring sight to be part of as I prepared for my morning surf.

As it turned out, I had the best surf that morning. The 'oldies' had inspired me not to wear my wetsuit so I felt so much more free and uninhibited surfing in my favourite bathers I'd bought in Byron Bay. Secretly, I was just pretending I was still surfing there in bathers only and my longboard – although it was a chillier Victorian morning! I felt alive, connected, focussed and powerful. I could feel my strength training in the gym was paying off as my paddling was more purposeful and I caught nearly every wave I paddled for. I was turning better and positioning myself on my longboard more eloquently to make the most of the wave's momentum. My mind was clear and I was surfing with pleasurable intent. I felt so happy, content, relaxed but yet still driven and energised at the same time. I love this paradoxical way of feeling. It is definitely me as my best self.

Do you know your 'why'?

Why do I get up so early and travel so far to surf? Why do I go out in freezing cold conditions? Why do I paddle out in crazy waves? Why do I never regret any of these moments?

Midlife is now the point in time where I can honestly say, it is not the how, when or where that is important – it is the WHY. For most of my life, I focussed on what I wanted, or what I thought I

Rediscovering Yourself: Defining Your WHY and Your passion

wanted. The WHY wasn't really a well thought out consideration. The problem with starting with the WHAT, is that I think I have discovered that it is a limiting construct and actually hard work. I feel my inner self requires me to fill her with what is most meaningful rather than focussing on what a specific outcome should be. Don't get me wrong, being goal-driven and outcome-focussed is what has given me wonderful aspects in my life. Without that mindset of focussing on my WHAT, I probably wouldn't have the education, career, financial and family achievements that I have now. I have all these tangible products in my present life that I'm proud of having worked for and I am enjoying what they bring to me. It's easy to be driven from the WHAT because it's easy to measure and easy to quantify through talking about what we own, what degrees we hold, what job titles we have had, what is our marital status and the list is ongoing. However, I still feel a sense of tiredness and heaviness when I look back and think about WHAT and HOW I have achieved everything thus far. To me, the HOW is what I need to do to get to the essence of my WHY. Moving forward, I now focus on my WHY. Ask yourself these questions:

Do you know WHY you do something?

WHY do you want to achieve that goal?

Can you describe your WHY?

The WHY should be our reasons for doing what we do and it's about what matters to you most. It is underpinned by our core values and is what we stand for, what we want to be known for and it is the something that is just waiting to burst out of you. Your WHY moving into your midlife should be (must be) the *passion* that has been forgotten about whilst you have been busy in life raising children, being educated, working in careers and jobs, caring for others, and again the list goes on... Your WHY is in your heart, in your soul and is that burning voice that is telling you now is the time to discover or redefine it for both yourself and for those around you. Permission granted!

It's time to flip the thinking and focus on the WHY. If you continue to focus on the WHAT, you'll still achieve wonderful things. However, after a period of time, if you sit back and reflect or you continue to feel tired and heavy whilst doing this, you will ask yourself, 'WHY am I doing this (still)?' You may have nagging feelings of unfulfillment, disengagement, a sense of apathy. This is creating a paradox in your mind as you think you are achieving all these wonderful milestones and outcomes and you should be feeling exhilarated and on top of the world – yet you're not. That's because, defining your WHY is so much harder than determining and doing your WHAT.

I was at a 'Women in Leadership Summit' in Melbourne and I was listening to a keynote speaker. She was describing her life journey from refugee status to now owing her own successful business. I was captivated by her story as it resonated so deeply with me. I'm not from refugee status but from migrant parents and am first generation Australian. She was describing her upbringing whereby education, building a career and creating a family were perceived as important values and milestones in her life. She talked about how she managed to 'tick off' all those achievements. I too am the same. However, she described herself as living this 'princess' life but still searching for 'something'. She had dissonance in her heart and discord in her soul. I had such a strong urge to stand up and say, 'Me too!' She finished her keynote by concluding that due to her need to build a substantial life in Australia having been a refugee, she was operating from her WHAT and not her WHY. I resonated with this so strongly because it is exactly how I have operated unknowingly as well. To this day, I often question myself as to why I am feeling disconnected, not fulfilled, displaced and yet I have absolutely everything in my life that should result in the opposite feelings. This is what I have been able to unpack in my search for my WHY:

Rediscovering Yourself: Defining Your WHY and Your passion

My WHY relates to my passions, purpose, visions, desires, drivers and intentions.

My WHAT relates to specific goals, objectives and measurable outcomes and achievable milestones.

My HOW relates to methods, strategy, approaches, ways of doing, plans and processes.

My WHEN relates to the timeframe for achieving my whats

Defining my WHY has been challenging because it is emotion-based and requires me to take the time to reflect on my true self and what is my true essence as a person (that is, who is the real me?). It's easy to operate in the WHAT as it's logical and driven by my thought processes, past experiences, what I'm comfortable with and doing what has worked in the past. It's almost a sense of auto pilot. It's also easy for me to operate in the HOW as this is my default of action, achieving, progressing, taking the accolades and rinse and repeat.

This chapter explores how to reconnect with your passions, values and dreams, letting go of what doesn't serve your best self and gives you permission to embrace the woman you've become in your 50s, with confidence and purpose. It's time to break down the silos and barriers between our mental and physical selves which exist between WHAT our goals are and WHY we really want them. Ponder that for a moment. It's time now in our lives to allow ourselves to indulge in and create what is possible and to take time to draw the big picture. The idea of doing this may seem daunting and it's easier to go about our lives focussing on the WHAT but I guarantee you, if you take the time to pause and discover your WHY, your life will take on a whole new path.

The 50s Compass

*It was a Thursday afternoon, and I was sitting at my computer in the open plan office. I was looking around and noting the 'vibe' of the room. Like me, some people were sitting at their computers staring into space, scrolling on their phones or squinting at the screen whilst clicking the mouse. Others were rummaging through handbags, sipping on stale coffee or talking quietly amongst themselves. I thought, this is not really the 'vibe' that lights me up. As I looked at the time and noted it was only 3pm, I took myself back to a conversation that I once had with Richard. When I came home complaining that I was bored with life and work was mundane, he replied that work was a necessary part of life, but what I needed to do was identify my **passion**. His explicit words were, 'Find that thing that you think about when you are totally bored at work, what is that thing? What's the thing that gets you fired up, excited and it's basically all that you think about?' I couldn't answer that question. I didn't have a 'thing'. This again was another catalyst which unknowingly led to me discovering my WHY.*

I'm very inquisitive, curious, adventurous and ridiculously spontaneous. So, after my episode of experiencing the mundane office life once too often and concerning myself that I couldn't actually answer the question about what my 'thing' was – I booked a trip to Nepal. It was the turning point in my quest to re-discovering my passions during my midlife.

As I sat at Melbourne airport, I began to journal and draw. Finally, in my late 40s, I was able to step out of motherhood, work life and every other responsibility that life has, to take 10 days to myself to let my brain breathe again. I often read back over my Nepal journal and wonder how I survived the chaos and hectic pace that was occurring at that point in time. I had 10 days to myself in the Himalayas to decompress, recharge and re-focus.

Kathamandu was alive and bustling. It was a somewhat eclectic regional town nestled in a valley overlooked by the awe-inspiring

Rediscovering Yourself: Defining Your WHY and Your passion

Himalayas. I couldn't get over the vastness of these mountains and the emotions that arose in me every time I looked up at them. One evening I was strolling through the narrow cobblestoned streets. There was such an integration of ancient culture, rich history and an urban way of living. It was a palette of colours from the iconic prayer flags, to the gemstones on display, through a variety of hiking apparel that hung from the store rooflines in order the attract the next adventurous hiker. I could feel an intense sense of tradition and energy that seemed to captivate me as I strolled these streets. My senses were being ignited and I was finally beginning to feel alive from within.

Those who know me well, know that I will strike up a conversation with anyone. Being alone in Nepal and wandering those intrepid streets didn't deter me at all. I stepped into a fabric shop, lured by the beautiful colours of the fabrics and the strong sense of incense burning. I was met cheerfully by a young woman probably around the age of 20. She invited me into her shop and in no time, we were sitting out the back enjoying a cup of freshly brewed Nepali tea. We began to share stories, as most women do and it felt like I had been here all my life. I told her about my nursing days and that I was a neonatal intensive care nurse. She didn't understand what this was, but when I described that I cared for very premature babies who had entered the world sometimes 10 weeks too early, her eyes nearly popped out of her head. She described to me that she was the first girl in her family and that nursing was something that she always wanted to do. Her family, much like many of those in Nepal, were not financially affluent and a career in nursing would only ever be a pipe dream. She told me that her father wanted her to concentrate on getting married and building a family. The family's expectation was that she would be married and then work in the family fabric shop within the next few years.

As I retell this story, I actually have tears welling in my eyes. Unfortunately, I couldn't do much to make the dream for this young girl to become a nurse a reality, but what I could do is listen to the emotions and thoughts that were erupting in myself. This was where I began to re-discover one of my passions in my late 40s. The encounter that I had with this young girl, in what was such a spiritual and emotive country, propelled me to recognise that mentoring and advocating for young women was indeed one of my passions. I was beginning to tap into my true essence of what really made me feel live.

To this day I continue to live this particular passion through my work. I lead a predominantly female team and always ensure that I have a young female who is early in her career as part of my team. I work closely with these young women to guide them and open career opportunities for them. My heart fills with warmth, pride and gratitude as I work with them and see them grow and develop. My greatest sense of pride, is when they have the confidence and courage to seek new employment or higher roles and to successfully negotiate their own salary during their contract stage. This reiterates to me that my passion for mentoring and supporting early career females is alive and present in my working life during my 50s.

I pose a question to you; what are you passionate about?

It's actually okay if you can't answer this. Often, by this stage of our lives we have suppressed our passions for so long that it's difficult to bring them to the surface and vocalise them. Sometimes I still find it difficult to articulate my passions but I definitely know the feeling from the inside when I am doing them. For the past 25 years I have been very busy navigating life and raising four children. None of those commitments are finishing any time soon, but amongst all of this, I needed to find my **passion** in order to create my WHY.

Most of the time we are not pursuing our passion because of the narrative in our head. We constantly come up with excuses such

Rediscovering Yourself: Defining Your WHY and Your passion

as, 'I don't know what my passion is, I don't have time, I don't have enough money to do it' and the list goes on. Therefore, it's not about the excuses anymore, it's about making it a priority and an intentional process to reaffirm your **passions**. Time is one thing that will never stand still and if you continue to waste more time procrastinating on finding your passion, you are missing out on the energy, joy and fulfillment that you will have to do more with your time.

Some reflection questions to guide in reigniting your passion

Take some time to find a quiet space, make it comfortable and take a moment to clear your mind. The following questions are suggested reflections that you may like to journal and write your answers to stimulate your thinking towards reigniting your passion.

Self-reflection and values
1. What activities make me lose sense of time and feel fully immersed?
2. During my younger years, what did I love doing the most?
3. What are my values and how can I bring these more into my life?
4. When do I feel truly alive and invigorated, and what am I doing in those moments?

What's holding me back?
5. What is the voice saying in my head that is holding me back from pursuing my passions?
6. Am I prioritising daily obligations over enjoyment? If so, how can I shift this dial?
7. What fears or words of apprehension come up when I think about going after my passion and how can I reframe this narrative?

How do I move towards my passions?
8. What is one small action that I can do today to reconnect with something that I love?
9. How can I bring more of my passions into my daily life?
10. Who will support me and keep me accountable in doing this? Who inspires me and how can I spend more time with them?

What does my big picture look like?
11. If I could create my ideal day/week/month/year, what would it look like?
12. When my passions are reignited, how are the other areas in my life improved such as work, relationships, health and mindset?
13. How do I want to be remembered and how does my passion contribute to this?

There are some beautiful words that I often draw upon from inspirational females. Here's a great quote that I love:

"The biggest adventure you can take is to live the life of your dreams." Oprah Winfrey

Oprah's words are a powerful reminder that by focussing on and pursuing what truly excites you, you wil undoubtedly be undertaking the greatest journey of all.

It's a task to identify your passions, but the next step is the commitment to yourself to implement them into your daily life. I've thought long and hard about this and realised that without a true commitment to yourself, the daily grind will continue to seep into your precious life. Here are some practical strategies to support with making your passions a meaningful part of your routine.

Rediscovering Yourself: Defining Your WHY and Your passion

1. Prioritise time for your passion
- Schedule a dedicated time in your diary/calendar to pursue and act on your passion, just like you would a family or work commitment
- Small bites or micro chunks, even just 15-30 minutes scheduled will make a difference

2. Assimilate passions into your daily routine
- If you love creativity, weave this into your day by playing the piano, drawing or journalling for a small portion of your day
- If you love physical movement, choose daily activities that excite you like walking, weight lift/gym sessions or dancing

3. Connect with like-minded people
- Join clubs or online groups that align with your passion
- Identify those who inspire you and follow their Instagram or socials
- Surround yourself with those who resonate with your passion

4. Leverage your passion into a growth/income opportunity
- Educate yourself by taking courses, workshops or read books that deepen your knowledge about your passion
- Explore if your passion could transform into a side hustle or career shift

5. Integrate your passion into existing responsibilities
- Share your passions with your family/children/partner and involve them
- Invite your passion into your workday, such as a walk during lunchtime, gym workout before or after work, starting new initiatives at work such as a book/journal club, lunch and learn sessions

6. Let go of procrastination and just start
- There is no perfect time to begin; just begin where you are and with what you have
- Nothing will ever be perfect, so just take a small step

7. Reevaluate and readjust
- Regularly check in with yourself and ask: does this still excite me? Am I feeling still energised by this??
- Be prepared to change and realign your passions as they develop and you continue to evolve

'Are you seriously going away again Mum?' I love this question asked by my 19-year-old son – to which I always answer, 'Yes!'

You see, at the age of 51, my passion is surfing and skateboarding. I know it may sound ridiculous and even insanely childlike, but I actually don't care. These are my passions. I love my children, my family, my career and I take these aspects of my life extremely seriously with full commitment and responsibility. However, surfing and skateboarding are my passions and these are what I have been alluding to throughout this chapter.

Imagine this scene... the waters are crystal, clear blue, there is nothing in sight except dotted islands of land spattered with palm trees and over water villas. There is not cloud in the sky as the plane turns towards its descent into Mali airport. I cannot believe that I am about to land in the Maldives, with my eight-foot foamie surfboard and my 15-year-old daughter in tow. For those of you who know surfing, you will know that the Maldives and foamie surfboards are a little incongruent. The Maldives is for somewhat more advanced surfers, and foamie surfboards are for somewhat beginner surfers! This didn't concern me, as firstly, I had no idea about this at the time of commencing this trip and secondly, I had my daughter with me, whom I love dearly and my surfboard, which is what I am passionate about.

Rediscovering Yourself: Defining Your WHY and Your passion

We had an incredible 10-day surf trip in the Maldives. I challenged myself beyond my expectations by sitting in the line up amongst experienced surfers, many of whom were loud Russians and Americans and I felt completely out of my depth. I caught about two waves for the entire trip because they were extremely fast and I learnt very quickly that if I didn't exit the wave in a timely and safe way, I'd be washed up well onto the coral reef. Therefore, I continued to go out every day and sit in the line up, but chose to watch from the shoulder and spend my time diving from my surfboard under the water to swim among the magical wonderland of tropical fish that was just below.

Another quick anecdote I'd like to share is the time I took myself to Byron Bay on yet another surf trip. It was a fabulous eight days full of exploring the unknown breaks around Byron and really pushing myself out of my comfort zone. It was the first time I surfed a left-hand wave and it was the first time that a small-sized shark (I swear by it) swam directly under my board. But this wasn't the highlight of my trip. The highlight was a couple of conversations that I had with a lovely young lady and this pint-sized 'kid' at the Byron Bay skate park!

When unable to surf, I love getting out on what is called a surf skate. It's a skate board that is specifically designed to help with surfing techniques. I love being able to cruise on it and carve gently along a path or more so, I love going to a skate park and 'pretending' that I'm still young enough to mix it with the 'skate crew'. During this Byron trip, I didn't have my surf skate with me, but because I'm so obsessed with my passion of surfing and skating, I couldn't help but take myself for a drive and sit around at the skate park one evening. Before long, I had struck up a conversation with this young lady who asked if I skated. She was a solo traveller from Canada and lent me her board to try out. She was impressed by my ability to navigate the terrain and we had a lovely exchange about our travelling stories. Whilst I sat watching her gliding so gracefully in the bowl (obviously she was a longboard surfer girl), I was suddenly aware of this tiny little child standing next to me. He was all of the age of five and stood no taller than knee height. He was ladened with helmet, knee pads, elbow pads and of course skateboard in hand. He promptly said to me, 'Can you drop in?' He had my unequivocal attention. This was our exchange:

Kid: 'Can you drop in?'

Me: 'Are you serious? No way. I'm like 50 years old.'

Kid: 'It's not hard, watch me.'

And with that, he dropped into the bowl and joined the young girl I was watching, gliding effortlessly on their boards. I could not wipe the smile off my face. As is the culture at skate parks, everyone is there following their passion for skating and what absolutely filled my heart that evening, was the fact that despite that I was probably five to ten times the ages of these young ones, they had no hesitation in chatting and connecting with me. They filled my soul and organically gave me their youthful energy that I still carry around to this day.

Rediscovering yourself and igniting your passions is all about unlocking and uncovering the parts of you that have been lying dormant or have been set aside along the busy path we call life. It's about embracing change and discovering the reasons for doing what we do and what matters most; that is our WHY. I hope throughout this chapter, there have been some practical tips and actions that you can put into place straight away. Don't underestimate the power that you have to create a life that feels vibrant, fulfilling and uniquely yours. So, go after what lights you up, lean into what fuels your soul and surround yourself with those that make you smile – it could be the pint-sized kid at the skate park!

Rediscovering Yourself: Defining Your WHY and Your passion

Do you want to keep your physical strength, energy and resilience at a healthy level whilst maintaining a sense of emotional regulation and spiritual connectedness?

Chapter 2

Thriving in Your 50s: Physical, Emotional and Spiritual Vitality

I preface this chapter with the fact that whilst I am a registered nurse, I am not a qualified nutritionist, exercise physiologist, personal trainer or the like. My intention throughout this chapter is to share some practical tips of what works for me. I am curious about supplements and I have included narrative around the ones that spark my interest personally. I note that everyone has a different view on health and wellbeing, so what I address here is purely from my own interests.

The 50s Compass

After I turned 50, I found a shift in my mindset and really started to prioritise physical strength. I didn't realise that as we age, our *oestrogen levels naturally decline* and this has negative effects on bone density as well as mood, sleep and menopausal symptoms. **Oestrogen** plays a role in maintaining lean muscle mass and as the levels drop, muscle protein synthesis declines leading to sarcopenia (age-related muscle loss). This obviously leads to decreased muscle strength and can really start to affect daily movements such as walking, climbing, balancing and lifting. The inevitable decreasing of oestrogen also contributes to fat accumulation around the abdomen and this, as I know from my nursing days, is a precursor to heart disease, type 2 diabetes and even certain cancers. Our bone density is also affected by decreasing oestrogen because cells that breakdown bone (osteoclasts) are more activated and this leads to osteopenia and osteoporosis. We are then more prone to fractures especially in the spine, hips and wrists as we age. Not a good sign for me, because at the age of 50, I still love to skateboard! You may be noticing joint pain and stiffness during midlife. That's because oestrogen has anti-inflammatory properties and as it declines we begin to feel these symptoms. I wasn't aware that oestrogen supported mitochondrial function which impacts energy levels. This is why we may be experiencing more fatigue and tiredness during midlife. It's also more difficult to bounce back and recover from workouts as we age, because oestrogen is necessary for muscle repair and recovery.

So, doesn't that all sound like doom and gloom? The inevitable decline in oestrogen has such a vast impact on our health and wellbeing. Once I discovered this, I made a quick but strong commitment to regular strength training, exercise, proper nutrition and rest. However, I'm also committed to nurturing my emotional regulation and spiritual connectedness. I'm finding that by implementing a couple of 'non-negotiables' into my life, my physical health has improved which is supporting my emotional balance, improving my mood and fostering a sense of inner peace.

Thriving in Your 50s: Physical, Emotional and Spiritual Vitality

I'm also staying spiritually connected by spending time in the ocean and simply taking more moments of stillness in my days – this significantly helps to ground and clarify my thoughts as I continue to navigate life's challenges. These deliberate commitments are 'non-negotiable' to me and are creating a harmonious flow that is enabling me to work with hormone hiccups, thrive physically, emotionally and spiritually whilst building the resilience I need to take into midlife and beyond.

Here's a snapshot of my non-negotiables:

- ✓ Progressive weight training 2-3 times a week
- ✓ Taking supplements
- ✓ Quarantined quiet time
- ✓ Weekly and quarterly surfing session/trips
- ✓ Tracking my nutritional intake daily

Implementing these non-negotiables into my life has been a game-changer. Just by making these adjustments and telling myself that these are the foundations for my future life, here are the differences I feel:

Before	After
👎 Irritable	👍 Emotionally regulated
👎 Lethargic	👍 Calm
👎 Mental fogginess	👍 Energised
👎 Physically heavy	👍 Strong
👎 Unhappy with my physique	👍 Happy to look in the mirror
👎 Overwhelmed	👍 Excited about life

Strength Training and Regular Exercise

I am by no means a certified personal trainer or fitness coach, however my nursing practice has given me an insight into health, fitness and wellbeing. Like many of you, I follow an array of Instagram people and I take snippets of their information and weave into my life what works for me – hence the formula above.

One key element is progressive weight training. It's especially beneficial in midlife as it helps to maintain muscle mass, bone density and overall strength which are key elements to staying active as we age. As the metabolism naturally slows down, resistance training enhances this as it increases lean muscle which helps manage weight gain and supports with joint health. Beyond the physical benefits, strength training improves mental resilience by releasing endorphins, reduces stress and enhances confidence. By making this a non-negotiable and consistently challenging the body with progressive overload, midlife will be taken on with more energy, improved posture, confidence and who would have thought – a new spring in your step!

I use an AI tool on a paid subscription to guide and track my weights. This keeps me motivated and committed. I take body composition measurements monthly to see my progress. I journal these and my thoughts in a wellness journal. I go the gym 2-3 times a week but at flexible times to suit my mood and schedule. I engage and pay a nutritionist for a 6-8 week time period once or twice a year to keep my diet on track and body composition moving. I use an app on my phone to track my daily habits.

Embracing progressive weight training, or resistance training into midlife is one of the most powerful ways to maintain strength, energy and overall wellbeing. It will preserve your bone health and muscle mass and enhance your confidence, resilience and mental clarity. By making this a consistent part of your midlife,

Thriving in Your 50s: Physical, Emotional and Spiritual Vitality

you will move with more ease, prevent injury and sustain a strong body composition. Midlife isn't the time to slow down – it's an opportunity to build a stronger, healthier foundation for the future.

Nutrition and Healthy Eating

Again, I am not a qualified nutritionist or dietary expert, but I can share what works for me and my 'pearls of wisdom' that I have collected along the way.

It was my 50th birthday and I had a wonderful afternoon at my home. I had invited my close friends over for champagne and wood fire pizzas. We took so many beautiful photos and there was true happiness in my smile. To anyone who was there, I seemed really quite happy and content with my life and my appearance.

Shortly after my 50th birthday, I took a trip to Western Australia and hired a campervan to drive from Perth to Exmouth. It was an amazing adventure and there are fabulous photos of me posing in the clear waters of Shark Bay, snorkelling with manta rays on the Ningaloo Reef and even lazing about on the idyllic Shell Beach. Again, true happiness in my smile.

When I look back at those photos, I can see a radiant face, brown tanned skin and what looks like someone who is living their best life. On the surface I was, yet inside, I was not happy with the way I looked, I felt heavy, I yearned for a more muscular physique and this was the ball and chain that was holding me back.

I took a long hard look in the mirror and decided I wasn't happy with what I saw. Those of you who know me, know that I'm a natural gal who doesn't fuss over appearance with glitz and glam. I am, though, a gal who knows that beauty does come from within and at that point in my life, when I looked in the mirror and at those photos from my Western Australian trip, I wasn't feeling my inner beauty. That's all ok. I have a healthy approach to my appearance and never seek to look like a Victoria Secret's model. Having said that, I wouldn't mind looking like Elle McPherson back in her day!

So, in addition to committing to 2-3 days of progressive weight training, I also committed to changing my body composition through proper nutrition and healthy eating. These two commitments go hand in hand and can't work in isolation. I engaged the knowledge of a professionally trained nutritionist and worked with him for an eight-week period. This was a wise investment of my time and money. It provided me with expert knowledge and accountability to an external person. During this time, my body composition improved but more so, I gained new knowledge, behaviours and discipline that I could take with me. Of course, we all tend to go off track and that again is ok. The difference for me now in midlife is that I recognise this early and again take meaningful actions to ensure that my body composition doesn't get too out of control. For me, it requires me to re-engage with the nutritionist to ensure that I am keeping up with healthy habits. Don't think that all of this has to be done alone. Explore your support options such as experts, programs and AI tools. There's a price point and support mechanism suitable to any of us.

Healthy nutrition is essential for women in midlife as it supports hormonal balance and overall energy and wellbeing. As we approach midlife, the body undergoes changes like menopause, slowing of metabolism, decreased muscle mass and hormonal shifts. It's therefore important to shift our way of eating and prioritise nutrient-dense food. Protein, protein, protein... as it maintains muscle strength. Healthy fats support brain function and hormone production and fibre assists in digestion and heart health. Lots of water for adequate hydration in addition to micronutrients like calcium, magnesium and vitamin D are all important for bone health and reducing our risk of osteoporosis as we age.

Thriving in Your 50s: Physical, Emotional and Spiritual Vitality

Adaptogens and supplements are things that I began to consider in midlife. Prior to this, I never took much notice of them and seemed to just put up with some symptoms which were beginning to impact my wellbeing. Every menstrual cycle, I found that I was becoming more and more irritable with a flat mood. This was beginning to impact my relationships with my children, work and myself. I therefore began to look at adaptogens and supplements. I found information about adaptogens such as ashwagandha which can help the body adapt to stress, reduce fatigue and improve resilience. I also found information that evening primrose oil can ease menstrual and menopausal symptoms such as mood swings and irritability. Other supplements like magnesium, omega-3 fatty acids and vitamin B can support brain health, muscle function and energy levels. Vitamin D and calcium supplements may also support the maintenance of bone density as we age.

Phytoestrogens was another word that took my interest as I started to really concentrate on my nutrition into midlife. I know that as menopause approaches our oestrogen levels begin to decline and this has negative effects on bone density as well as mood, sleep and menopausal symptoms. I'd highly recommend doing deeper research into the effects of decreasing oestrogen. I was curious as to how I could somehow support my body through diet as the oestrogen began to decline. That's where I found some insightful information on phytoestrogens. Again, this is not advice from a qualified nutritionist and I'm not going to cite academic studies; it's purely information that I have come across and applied snippets of into my life. I would encourage you to look at some academic literature around phytoestrogens as it's a whole other world out there and extremely interesting.

Phytoestrogens are also known as dietary oestrogen and are naturally occurring plant compounds that can function in a similar way to oestrogen that we produce in our bodies. The sources of phytoestrogens are widespread in Asian regions and have many health benefits from heart health, bone and skin health and the immune system. I have read that there are four types of phytoestrogens; isoflavones, stilbene, coumestan and lignin. Again, consult some academic literature for deeper information on this – it's fascinating.

We all get caught up in the Instagram hype of what to eat, what not to eat, what to wear, best places to go and the list goes on. One buzz phrase that I had been hearing a lot is – eat edamame, it's really good for you. I actually tried these and they are a little bit addictive. I found a bit of therapeutic pleasure in squeezing their pod and eating them from there, enjoying their crunch! It was a bit of a novelty. Little did I know that these little cuties are actually a type of soybean and are rich in phytoestrogen and protein. So now, I replace munching on potato chips with munching on edamame.

As we know, phytoestrogens are a form of dietary oestrogen that we can get from food. I found that there are many sources from which we can obtain these plant-based nutrients:

The best dietary sources of phytoestrogens are:

1. **Flaxseeds:** are small golden brown seeds rich in lignans. You can sprinkle them on a variety of dishes, bake them into biscuits or breads or even blend them into smoothies
2. **Soy:** is rich in vitamins, phytoestrogens known as isoflavones, protein and minerals. It can be processed into many plant-based products such as tofu and tempeh and can also be enjoyed whole as edamame (I never knew I was eating soy when enjoying these!).
3. **Dried Fruits:** are nutrient dense, sweet and easy as an 'on the go' snack. The ones highest in phytoestrogens are dates, prunes and dried apricots. They're also full of fibre.
4. **Sesame Seeds:** these are little fibre-packed seeds that can be sprinkled into many dishes and are commonly used in

Asian cuisine. They are a strong source of phytoestrogen and can add a unique crunch and nutty flavour.
5. **Peaches:** this sweet fruit is high in phytoestrogens known as lignans and also many other vitamins and minerals.
6. **Berries:** particularly strawberries and blackberries are loaded with vitamins, minerals, fibre and phytoestrogens
7. **Tofu:** contains concentrated amounts of phytoestrogens known as isoflavones. Tofu has the highest levels of isoflavone of any soy produce, however, soy milk is still a good source.
8. **Tempeh:** is made from fermented whole soy beans and is an excellent source of protein, prebiotics, vitamins, minerals and phytoestrogens known as isoflavones. It is a common meat replacement in a vegetarian diet

Because of their complex actions, the effects of phytoestrogens remains a topical conversation. I personally found it very useful to browse the literature and broaden my knowledge on the effects it can have throughout midlife. My takeaway is that I incorporate these into my diet now with a little bit more intention and knowledge than I previously had.

Being the mother to three sons, I obviously went on a unique journey in my parenthood. I often felt like the only hormone in the house was testosterone! Their father was such a good role model and influence on their health and physical wellbeing. He was strongly dedicated to their football games but more so to their training and ensuring that their young developing bodies were in the best physical shape to play such a high contact sport. He would work with them in the park next door doing physical training and running drills and I loved watching all of them working and training together like this. My boys weren't 'gym junkies or gym rats' by any means, nor was their father, but they did take their weight sessions in the gym seriously. During this phase, my kitchen cupboards were laden with bottles and jars of pre-workout, creatine, amino acids and assorted protein powders. Funnily enough, at the time I was probably in my 30s and didn't take any notice of these supplements and what their actual functions were.

It's only now, in my early 50s, that I'm following up on my interest in body building and body composition. It's an interest that has been there in the background but during the hustle and bustle of my 30s I didn't take any notice regarding the actions of these supplements. I am loving that I now have the space and time in my life to research these and work in a more focussed way with my nutritionist to learn about these supplements. We're never too old to learn and I am following my interest in learning about these.

Creatine was a supplement that always seemed to have a place in the kitchen cupboard, yet I really didn't understand what its function was. It has a reputation that body builders and gym junkies would take this to maintain the energy supply to the muscles whilst they were under strain during a workout. As I began reading more and researching the benefits to taking creatine in midlife, I found that it isn't just for gaining muscle mass for stereotypical body builders. It can play a significant role in building strong muscles and assisting with longevity into later life. So naturally, even if we aren't professional bodybuilders, it may be something worth knowing more about.

If you're reading this, thinking that you want to lose weight rather than bulk up with big muscles, then know that creatine isn't a supplement that will bulk you up. It's a chemical that is already naturally found in the body and its main responsibility is to provide energy for muscles to negate feeling weak or experiencing cramping. Creatine works by increasing the body's store of phosphocreatine which is the molecule that helps produce adenosine triphosphate (ATP). You may be getting some form of PTSD now because for those of us who took Year 12 Physical Education, we learnt that ATP is the primary source of energy for your cells particularly during short burst of exercise. This is why creatine is a favourite amongst weightlifters and bodybuilders.

Unfortunately, midlife means that our muscles and tissues will begin to naturally weaken and recovery after exercise becomes harder. As women, we know that the onset of perimenopause and menopause means that our oestrogen levels also naturally drop and this negatively affects muscle elasticity. From what I have read, creatine can help with slowing down these processes when combined with regular exercise, particularly strength-based training. So again, try as best you can to engage in some sort of progressive strength-based training and investigate supplementing muscle health with creatine to make this type of training more manageable.

If you're like me and love a good flick through the academic literature, you'll soon come across articles that demonstrate that creatine can have a positive effect in the reduction of inflammation, decrease soreness and prevent injury, which are all concerns that we face as we enter into perimenopause and menopause. There is also interesting information to be found in relation to creatine and its influence on reducing brain fog. Yes, that's exciting to hear. I've read that the biggest percentage of creatine is stored in your skeletal muscles and the remaining amount is stored in your brain. Therefore, by adding creatine as a supplement to your routine, there may be the added benefit to brain health as well as muscle health, enabling us to boost our muscle mass plus our cognitive processing and functionality.

It might be worth investigating the benefits of creatine with a certified health practitioner if this is something that resonates with you.

Essential amino acids are another element that spark my curiosity. There is always a conversation about what are they, how they work and what the difference is between essential amino acids (EAA) and creatine. Again, I found this a fascinating topic to research and learn more about.

Amino acids are the building blocks of proteins and we need them for vital processes such as building protein, hormones and neurotransmitters. They are organic compounds made up predominantly of hydrogen, carbon, nitrogen and oxygen. Apparently, our body needs 20 different amino acids to grow and function optimally, however of these 20, only 9 are classified as essential. Interestingly, although our body can make nonessential amino acids, it cannot make essential amino acids and we must obtain these from our diet. Not sure what Mother Nature was thinking here, but I guess that is why a healthy varied diet is important.

The best way we can obtain EAAs through diet is via animal proteins such as meat, eggs and poultry. For the plant-based eaters, EAAs are found in soy products such as edamame and tofu and these contain all 9 EAAs. That is, they are 'complete' protein sources which is very good to know. Therefore, if we eat protein, our bodies break it down into amino acids and then uses them for the various processes such as muscle growth, neurotransmission and regulating hormone functions.

There is a plethora of academic literature that discusses the relationship between midlife and amino acid supplements. It can be beneficial to maintaining muscle mass and supporting overall health. As our muscle protein synthesis decreases with age, supplementing with EAAs can help to combat sarcopenia (age-related muscle loss) and improve muscle strength. Therefore, it would be useful to investigate the literature relating to EAA supplementation on muscle preservation, improved muscle protein synthesis, combating sarcopenia, enhancing exercise performance and even contributing to blood sugar control.

Thriving in Your 50s: Physical, Emotional and Spiritual Vitality

Again, I found this topic fascinating, however it's important to take into consideration that every individual is different, the potential side effects of any supplement and to always consult with a professional health expert before starting any supplement regime.

In summary, a balanced, nutrient-rich diet not only fuels our body but enhances mood, mental clarity and supports us to thrive in this transformative stage of life. My personal reflection is that it's well worth consulting with exercise and nutrition experts to formulate an individual plan that will work for you. In my mind, this is money well spent.

Emotional and Spiritual Vitality

"The feminine energy is fluid, creative and intuitive. It does not force; it flows." – Unknown

This is a section that really lights up my soul. It gives me a sense of urgency, happiness and excitement as I write. That's because it is all about feminine energy and some goddess archetypes that I just love continuing to learn about. I'm hoping that by sharing this with you, it resonates and provides you with an opportunity to consider other ways of approaching aspects in your life.

I share with you the 'pearls of wisdom' that relate to feminine energy and masculine energy, not the stereotypical construct of what it means to be a man or a woman, boy or girl. We all have a mixture of both feminine and masculine energy within us, however if you are female you typically operate more in your feminine energy and if you are balanced in this, there should be a harmonious state of flow. Conversely, if you are male, you operate more in your masculine energy. Healthy relationships with others and with yourself feel 'easy' when there is the correct balance between these two types of energies.

Thriving in Your 50s: Physical, Emotional and Spiritual Vitality

Feminine energy has the characteristics of flow, creativity and nurture. It has attributes of faith, empathy, imagination and inspiration. Take a moment to pause here. Can you relate to any of these? As women, we are powerful creators and communicators. This is because feminine energy embodies qualities of receptivity, compassion and inner wisdom which allows for deep connection with ourselves and with others. Feminine energy nurtures and heals and embraces softness without weakness. Perhaps that is why many caring occupations such as nursing are dominated by females. Intuition is also very present within feminine energy and guiding through feeling rather than logic is present. It is an energy that holds creativity and expression and enables manifestations through intention rather than force. Therefore, if you are operating predominantly within your feminine energy there will be a strong sense of harmony, self-awareness and a presence of love and authenticity.

Masculine energy is more action-orientated and structured, much in contrast to the feminine which thrives in flow, adaptability and contours with life's natural cycles. Masculine energy embodies qualities of strength, discipline and logic. It holds strong to focus, determination and the ability to act decisively often moving forward with confidence and resilience. Feminine energy flows and adapts, yet masculine energy creates boundaries, provides stability and is always looking to protect and build. This energy values independence, problem-solving and leadership and is often displayed as ambition, courage and a strong sense of purpose. It can seem quite assertive and directional, yet balanced masculine energy offers elements of pause and reflect which can lead to wisdom rather than force. When flowing together with feminine energy, it creates a dynamic combination of power, action and presence.

How does feminine and masculine energy affect you?

Can you think of a time when your feminine and masculine energies have been out of alignment? This could be right now. If you are operating too much in your masculine energy you may be feeling quite rigid, trapped and your creativity and expression is felt to be blocked. You may seem to be having a difficult time expressing your needs or adapting to change. Equally, if you are operating too much from your feminine energy, you could be too mothering and taking on other people's problems, people pleasing and being overly forgiving, hence not holding your boundaries and space for yourself. You may also be finding that you are lacking productivity, pondering too much, procrastinating and you may be looking for others to help you out.

There was a period in my working career whereby I took a secondment into another department. The department I left was predominantly female, mostly mid-level career women and the focus of the work was centred on the health system. Reflecting back, during that time I was engaged and focussed in my work, I found it not too difficult, and there wasn't any disharmony that I can remember. I felt quite balanced. I took a 12-month secondment into another department to further my learning. Wow – what a time. It was a male-dominated workforce of both early-career and mid-career males. The females who were in this department were strong, forthright and I felt, quite non-nurturing. It was an entirely different way of working. Meetings were all very formal, projects and tasks were very tightly overseen by senior staff. The way in which people spoke to each other was very directive and non-emotional. As opposed to a health focus, this department had a focus on law enforcement. During this time, I felt small, somewhat scared and minimised. I felt my voice didn't matter and to be honest, I was petrified of making a mistake as I knew there would be a consequence. I vividly remember and can still feel the emotions of shame as I was publicly humiliated in a large meeting by the Executive Director. Ironically, she was a female and utilised all her masculine energy to openly pinpoint a lapse in meeting a milestone in a project that I was undertaking. I have never forgotten that use of power and control towards me. An experience that I would never want anyone who values their feminine energy to be subjected to. Subsequently, as soon as the 12 months was finished, I left and returned to my substantive department. At the time, I had no idea why I felt such contrast between these two working environments. Now that I know more about feminine and masculine energy, I can reflect and validate my feelings. I was working in an environment that was excessively dominated by masculine energy. Now this is what may have been needed considering it was focussed on law enforcement; however, it was definitely not congruent to my way of working. So, I now know, that especially in a working environment, I need to be in a place that is more in line with feminine energy.

Balancing feminine and masculine energy involves doing activities that align to each energy's natural state of flow. Here are some activities that you may want to either bring into your life or do less of, in order to balance your energetic alignment.

Feminine Energy Activities (Creativity, Flow, Intuition, Nurturing)

1. **Journaling and Reflection:** take a beautiful journal and use it to write anecdotes from your day, express your emotions, jot down your dreams, provide words of wisdom, capture those pearls.
2. **Spending Time in Nature:** take your shoes off, walk on the beach, feel the grass, swim in the ocean, meander down that path, admire the sunrise or sunset, feel the wind and listen to those birds.
3. **Creative Expression:** pick up that paint brush, coloured pencils, pen and paint, draw and create an image, vision or picture of your mind. Play that musical instrument, write that song or even sing the tune that makes you feel alive.
4. **Dancing and Free Movement:** take that yoga or dance session, dance about your bedroom, pretend you are a tai-chi expert and move freely in a place that brings you peace, go to that festival or gig and purely dance.
5. **Self-Care and Sensory Experiences:** take that long bath, have the facial and massage, put fresh sheets on the bed,

light the fragrant candle, apply a scented body lotion, put fresh flowers in a vase and soak up their scent.
6. **Deep Conversations and Emotional Connection:** pick up the phone, meet for that coffee with a loved one or friend and engage with intention. Embrace or hug another and feel the energetic flow.
7. **Meditation and Breathwork:** take a guided meditation, create a space of stillness, listen to your breath, focus on your intuition.
8. **Surrender & Trust Exercises:** find a quiet space, write down what you are holding on to, list any fears, acknowledge your feelings, shift the focus from control to trust (I trust that everything is unfolding as it should be…).

Masculine Energy Activities (Discipline, Action, Structure, Strength)

1. **Strength Training and Exercise:** lift weights either in the gym or at home, martial arts or playing competitive sports. These don't have to be extreme as even mixed netball adds a mixture of competitiveness and intensity.
2. **Goal-Setting and Strategy Planning:** creating structured plans and setting clear goals. Perhaps use a framework such as SMART goals.
3. **Taking Initiative and Leadership:** make decisive decisions in a timely manner, lead projects and take initiative in setting the timeframes and deliverables, initiate change management or support and lead these initiatives.
4. **Problem-Solving and Logical Thinking:** play strategy board games, undertake structured learning and work within the frameworks, develop process flows.
5. **Challenging Yourself:** commit to an endurance task or activity, do an ice bath, step out of your comfort zone, try a new activity, step into the unknown.
6. **Setting Boundaries and Practicing Discipline:** saying no to taks that don't align with you, maintain a commitment or

focus, commit to routines and rituals, define your vision or purpose.
7. **Solo Time and Independence:** spend time by yourself without any distractions, take yourself away on a short trip, travel solo, go out for dinner alone, go to the movies alone, build your inner strength and resilience, focus on your mental clarity.

Hopefully you can see that there is a need for both feminine and masculine energy to be present within you. How much of each is an individual feeling. By listening to your body and your feelings, you will know if your energies are in alignment. Balancing both feminine and masculine energy in your daily life means uniting action with flow, structure with creativity and strength with receptivity. How do I do this? Here's a suggestion:

- ❁ Start the day with a structured routine (masculine) but allow for changes and move through this with flexibility and intuition (feminine)

- ❁ When making decisions throughout your day, use logic and strategy (masculine) while also listening to your emotions and intuition (feminine)

- ❁ Make sure you keep up your resistance or strength training (masculine) but balance this with self-care, rest, free movement, such as baths, stretching or yoga (feminine)

- ❁ In your relationships, assert boundaries (masculine) while fostering the deep emotional connections and communication such as active listening (feminine)

By consciously integrating both the feminine and masculine energies into your daily life, you hopefully will start to create a life that is energetic, driven and fulfilling which feels powerful yet peaceful. Go on – give it a try!

> *"The goddess within you is calling – will you answer?" – Unknown*

There is another element to emotional and spiritual vitality that I would love to share with you. It is that of archetypes. Feminine archetypes, especially the goddesses from mythology and spiritual traditions, have helped guide me throughout many challenging situations in my life. Whether that has been, giving birth (four times), navigating complex relationships, or even actually surviving a big wipe out in the surf. These serve as powerful symbols of wisdom, strength, transformation and resilience – qualities that are very important during midlife.

As we begin to navigate this stage, we may be confronted by shifts in identity (who am I as an empty nester, retiree, grandparent, divorcee, widow...), purpose (what do I stand for? what's my direction?), and energy (I'm feeling tired, depleted, not on track...). These archetypes offer guidance, inspiration and a deeper connection to your intuition and inner strength. They are an option for providing a powerful framework to understanding and embracing different aspects of your life. They can be useful in self-discovery, storytelling and personal development. I love them!

Here are some ways in which you could use feminine archetypes:

1. **Navigating Life Transitions:** they can help to navigate changes such as ageing, career shifts, personal transformations.
2. **Self-Discovery & Empowerment:** some of the archetypes can assist in recognising different facets of yourself. It could

be traits that align to nurture, independence or wisdom. Using archetypes as a guide can foster self-awareness and personal growth.
3. **Balancing Strength & Challenges:** the archetypes have strengths and shadows that can help cultivate a sense of balance. For example, the Lover is passionate but can struggle with co-dependency, the Warrior is strong but can resist vulnerability.
4. **Reclaiming Authenticity:** often we feel the pressure to fit into a societal norm. Archetypes can offer another way to embrace different expressions of femininity. This can be from independence and ambition to nurturing and sensuality, allowing for the letting go of any shame or inhibitions.

Feminine archetypes and mythological goddesses have introduced me to parts of myself that I had locked away and forgotten about...

Once I started doing some reading on this topic, I found it was a labyrinth of information. It was a whole other realm to knowing and I felt that I was connecting deeply with all that I found. Learning about the Divine Feminine and the Divine Masculine led me into the pathway of feminine archetypes and mythological goddesses. I listened intently to Sabrina Lynn and took elements of her work into my daily life. She spoke a language that pivoted around the magical parts that are buried within us, under the construct of day-to-day life and she offers many insights into how to reignite and connect with this part of self.

So what exactly is an archetype? It's somewhat like an avatar that is a universal symbol and represents basic patterns of behaviour, energy or aspects of your personality. They help us see and understand a lot about how and why we may do or feel certain things. The very famous Swiss psychologist, Carl Jung, introduced the concept of archetypes into psychology. He believed that the human mind contains, in his terms, a collective unconscious. Which means that we all have a deep layer in our psyche that is filled with inherited memories and ways of being. He created these archetypes from the collective unconscious which is thought to drive our thoughts, emotions and behaviours. Interestingly, Jungian psychology explored the specific archetypes related to gender. He described the feminine archetypes of; The Mother, The Lover, The Wise Woman, as expressing different parts of feminine energy, whilst the masculine archetypes; The King, The Warrior, The Magician, spoke to the masculine energy traits of a person.

Here are some feminine archetypes:

- ✿ **The Mother:** she is one of the most well-known archetypes and she represents nurturing, generosity, unconditional love and compassion. This archetype isn't limited to biological mothers per se, but represents all forms of caregiving and nurturing. The shadow side to The Mother is that she has the potential to become co-dependent or too pleasing and can wonder why she herself isn't taken care of.
    - **Examples of The Mother** – Demeter in Greek mythology, Mother Theresa, The Fairy Godmother and Mary Poppins.

- ✿ **The Maiden:** she represents youth, full potential and new beginnings. This archetype portrays the spirit of adventure, willing to learn, curiosity and innocence. She resonates closely with the Goddess of Spring in Greek mythology and she is full of growth, representing the start of a woman's journey. The shadow side of The Maiden is that she can sometimes take on a victim mentality and gives her power away to the saviour (usually a male).
    - **Examples of The Maiden** – Persephone in Greek mythology, Snow White, Cinderella and Beth from Little Women.

- ✿ **The Huntress:** she embodies independence, focus, drive and determination. She represents the free-spirited dimensions and the wild woman within. She is not confined by societal expectations and likes to live a life determined by her own ways. The shadow side of The Huntress is that she may build defences around her heart and become disconnected from her own deep emotional expressions. Sometimes, intimate and close relationships are difficult because she sees vulnerability as a weakness.
  - **Examples of The Huntress** – Artemis in Greek mythology, Lady Gaga, Wonder Woman and Serena Williams.

- ✿ **The Lover:** she represents passion, sensuality and emotional connectedness. She is playful and has a gift for creating beauty and seeing beauty within her life and surrounds. She embodies a deep and profound aspect of the feminine and has the ability to form intense connections and experiences life through her senses. She is driven by emotion more so than logic. Her shadow is that she can feel a strong need for external validation and holds a fear of rejection. The Lover needs to be aware of not falling into addictive patterns as she is strongly driven to experience pleasure.
  - **Examples of The Lover** – Aphrodite from Greek mythology, Marilyn Munroe, Baby from Dirty Dancing, Juliet from Romeo and Juliet and Scarlett O'Hara from Gone with the Wind.

- ✿ **The Queen:** she is regal, confident and embodies personal power and leadership. The Queen is focussed on building her life and radiates with confidence and divine feminine energy. Others look to her because of her self-assurance and ability to stay focussed. She also enjoys the finer things in life and being treated well. Her shadow is prone to becoming addicted to work, perfectionism and she can struggle with jealousy.

- **Examples of The Queen** – Hera, the wife of Zeus in Greek mythology, Queen Elizabeth II, Beyonce, Nancy Reagan and Daenerys from Game of Thrones.

✿ **The Wise Woman:** she represents wisdom and experience. She has lived through life's events and holds deep understanding and inner knowledge. She shares her wisdom to help others grow and is at peace with herself. The first documented Wise Woman archetype came from Greek mythology in the form of the Goddess Hecate. She can be depicted as a woman with three faces as Hecate had the ability to see into the past, present, and future. Her shadow side relates to a tendency to become cynical and manipulative. She needs to be aware of her controlling ability due to her knowledge.
- **Examples of The Wise Woman** – Athena from Greek mythology, Professor McGonagall from Harry Potter and Belle from Beauty and the Beast.

Archetype Mirror Activity: Meet Your Inner Feminine Forces

This is a fun activity that I've crafted to help you meet with your inner feminine archetypes that live within especially as you navigate midlife.

1. Meet the Archetypes:

The Mother – nurturing, generous, unconditional love and compassion

The Maiden – youthful, full of potential, new beginnings, spirit of adventure

The Huntress – independent, focussed, driven and determined

The Lover – passionate, creative, sensual, emotional vitality

Thriving in Your 50s: Physical, Emotional and Spiritual Vitality

The Queen – wise, self-assured, leads with grace

The Wise Woman – wisdom, experience, deep understanding, inner knowledge

2. Connecting with your archetype:

Which archetype feels most natural to you? Why?

Which one feels distant or underused? Why might that be?

Where in your life do you want to highlight and use these archetypes?

What would it feel like to embody some of these archetypes into your daily life?

3. Creating your archetype embodiment plan:

Choose one archetype to embody and use more fully over the next week.

Write three small practical or symbolic actions that you will take to action this archetype and make her come alive within you.

Assign this into your calendar against different days.

Example:

To embody the Huntress archetype; 'I will speak up and say no to a request that doesn't align with my values'.

To embody The Lover archetype; 'I will ask my partner to take me on a date and we can design this together'.

The 50s Compass

"I thought parenting got cheaper after they turned 18 – turns out they just text more expensive problems!" – Sarah Ong

Chapter 3

Guiding with Grace: Parenting Young Adult Children and Nurturing Grandchildren

"You have to prepare yourself for that moment, because they will leave and your job is to make sure they leave well – strong and independent and able. But man, it hurts." – Michelle Obama

The 50s Compass

I can literally still see myself and feel my emotions that spread through me in that toilet cubicle in the Neonatal Intensive Care Unit at the Royal Children's Hospital in the February of 2001. I worked a good part of my nursing career caring for other people's precious babies as a neonatal intensive care nurse. I was twenty-eight. The image that I am describing to you, relates to myself and my close friend and colleague at the time, Katie. We were both trying to get pregnant for the first time and this was a whole new experience for us. We were both adept at caring for other people's babies, who required such complex care, yet we were so naive and fresh faced when it came to our own lives and starting a family.

It was well into a night duty and I said to Katie something along the lines of – 'Hey I want to know if I am pregnant. It's killing me not knowing.' Mischievous as we were back then, she coaxed me into taking one of the pregnancy tests from the ward and sneaking off into the toilet cubicle to do it. Curiosity got the better of me, and of course I did it! After doing the classic – peeing on the stick – I waited and to my absolute horror/surprise/what the hell do I do now response, I stared wide eyed at two albeit faint lines. I rushed back to show her and the two of us were like giggling school girls. You need to remember, it's around 2am, there is stillness all around at the nurses' station and the neonatal ward is unusually quiet. Night duty does strange things to a person's mind...

I do pride myself on being somewhat academically smart, but when it comes to practical life, occasionally I am not so smart. I excitedly questioned the result with her – 'What does this mean, two lines, they're faint, I don't think it's accurate'. She says it's a proper pregnancy test that we use on patients and therefore the result is going to be accurate. I can't comprehend this in my mind and so I sneak in and take another test, rushing excitedly into the toilet cubicle again. Sure enough, two more lines indicating a positive result show up. I can still describe the feelings of happiness, overwhelming excitement, disbelief, confusion and uncertainty all

Parenting Young Adult Children and Nurturing Grandchildren

bundled into one. It's a moment in time that is never to be forgotten, the time that you discover you are pregnant with your first child. Just between you and me, I did do another three tests throughout the night as my practical life 'smarts' weren't really turned on! Apologies to the tax payer for using all those pregnancy tests back in 2001!

Now, I could write an entire book on all four of my beautiful children, each with their own unique and quintessential personalities. I had firmly planted in my mind, that life would give me two daughters. As we all know, the Universe has other ideas and I have been gifted three sons and one daughter. I will confess that I did keep trying for a girl until I got the third son. At this point, Katie and I were still creating our families and we were both up to three boys each. We did a somewhat rock, paper, scissors decision to try for a fourth and cross fingers and toes that we had girls. Well, you can guess the odds, at least one of us would have the girl. It was me. She has four amazing young men now and I love seeing them tower over her. As I write this book, I have three young men, ages 23, 21 and 19 and one blossoming daughter aged 16. This is a chapter whereby I want to offer the opportunity to reflect on what it's like evolving as a parent as our children continue to grow and we consider the likelihood that grandchildren may also enter into our realm.

The Evolving Role as a Parent

As we enter into our 50s there's a moment in our parenting role that we don't quite see coming. It happens slowly and organically, however I feel that this moment occurs when we least expect it. One moment, we seem to be busy packing lunchboxes, organising school uniforms, arguing about too much screen time and the next... you're standing in a quiet house, wondering what your grown children are currently doing, are they coming home for dinner and basically, when will you see them next?

The 50s Compass

The beautiful thing is that parenting doesn't end when our children become adults. It simply shifts. It takes on an energy that is softer and quieter. It's more about being a steady presence rather than a constant guide and instructor in their lives. And truthfully, as I write this book, I am in the midst of this transition in my parenting. I actually feel like I am now able to take a breath in my parenting and I am absolutely relishing in the fact that I am still a large part of my children's lives but they are less reliant on the day-to-day tasks that need doing for them.

When our children are small, we act like the CEO of their lives, constantly managing everything from mealtime to manners. It often feels relentless with no opportunity for the four weeks of annual leave we get from our work place. Oh, how as mothers being able to apply for that intrepid sick day would have been a blessing! Yet, as our children are now entering early adulthood, our parenting role changes and we are no longer their managers. We seek to become their mentors. Gently offering insights, wisdom and resisting the urge to micro manage their lives and their decisions.

More often than not, it's difficult to step aside from being their CEO as we see them heading towards a life lesson that we know will hurt. Broken hearts are always hard to mend and as a parent, are so difficult to watch happen to our children. But part of evolving as a parent in our midlife is to allow our grown up babies to face those hardships and bumps in their life road, knowing that they will grow stronger through the experience. The important thing here is to be there with a hug, a good meal or a 'you've got this and you're okay', when they need it most.

It was a Friday afternoon around 4.30pm. I was outside my garage door blowing leaves in the driveway with the leaf blower. Amidst the humming of the blower, I suddenly heard the slamming of the front door and quickly before my eyes was my eldest son, 21 at the time. He had a look of bewilderment in his eyes which were wide open and about to pop out of his head.

Parenting Young Adult Children and Nurturing Grandchildren

'Mum,' he yelled as he approached me. 'I've f$#3ed it!' were his words.

'F$#3ed what?' I asked trying not to sound too alarmed.

'My flight to Qatar! I'm supposed to be on it now not tomorrow. I have a connecting flight on to Paris. What am I going to do?'

At that exact moment, my heart sank. My big boy had saved for so long for this lifetime adventure. He was going overseas with his high school mates to spend a few months travelling around Europe. This had been his dream whereby every spare penny he worked tirelessly for had been put towards this trip. I immediately stopped my leaf blowing activity and asked him to calmly explain to me the situation.

For a child who studied so hard at school and received an Atar score most would dream about, this kid definitely lacks the street smarts of his brothers! He had organised himself so well, planned his destinations, accommodation and even organised the connecting flights single-handedly. But when it comes to simple things like remembering to take the passport or specifically in this case, remembering the date of the flight, my eldest baby can be somewhat remiss.

So, I step into Mother archetype and quickly put down the leaf blower to head inside with my distraught son at my heels. I ask him quietly for the flight details and his passport. He hands them over and I call the phone number to Qatar Airlines. My son watches on anxiously from across the kitchen table as I try in all my Motherly best to remain calm on the phone as I explain the situation. I even throw in a line about him only being 21 and that he had worked so hard to save for this trip. I put my 'please feel sorry for him' tone of voice on and explained that he had missed his flight from Melbourne to Qatar which departed half an hour ago whilst he was still in his bedroom at home and that he had a connecting flight to Paris as well.

You should have seen the relief on my face when the Qatar operator said, 'Sure I can reassign another flight for him, same time tomorrow and that will ensure that he still has his connecting flight'. Both my son and I breathed a huge sigh of relief. Just as I was about to bear my sincere gratitude for her assistance, she followed with the sentence, 'and that will be $2300 Australian dollars, how would you like to pay?' I nearly fell off my chair but to his credit, my poor boy handed over his credit card and paid for his mistake. It took all my strength not to step in and pay for him. This was a lesson he would never forget!

Balancing Influence With Independence

As our children enter into the vast expanse of adulthood, letting go and allowing them to step into this world doesn't mean stepping away. It's an opportunity for us as parents to begin to balance our influence with their evolving independence. It means giving space while we continue to stay connected. For me, it's about a mind shift and taking a different approach to my parenting. I am focussing on choosing trust over worry and presence over pressure.

Me as parent to young adult child: 'Hey what are you up to tonight, do you need dinner?'

Young adult child aged 19: 'Nah, the boys are coming over and we're making a doof stick for BTV'.

For those of you who have young adult children, this type of communication is filled with a breadth of information for you as a parent. Even though it literally consisted of two verbal sentences, I am now informed that my 19-year-old doesn't need food for the evening and is coming together with his friends to plan for their summer holidays which is consisting of them attending a music festival which I have never heard of. I confess, I did have to Google

Parenting Young Adult Children and Nurturing Grandchildren

'doof stick', and upon reading the eye-opening response I could feel the anxiety rising from my biggest toe to my chest!

My 19-year-old and his friends were planning to attend the Beyond the Valley Festival which is a well known multi-day music festival held in regional Victoria. The 'doof stick' is a large home made sign that is attached to a pole and decorated accordingly... It's used to help groups of friends find each other at music festivals. One might think that as a parent, I'd be pleased that my child was putting his fine art skills and creativity to good use in making this 'doof stick'. However, when the themes of these sticks centre around nothing but recreational and party drug use at festivals, I had really mixed feelings!

So here I reiterate what I have written previously about re-framing my parenting focus to choosing trust over worry and presence over pressure. My innate instincts were of course to start a rant about not going to this festival as it was so far away, there would be way too many people, what were they going to eat and drink, how were they going to sleep, what were they going to wear and more importantly were they going to take recreational drugs... oh my goodness this is going to send me to an early grave. I absolutely refrained from any of that narrative to the 19-year-old and instead asked some general questions and showed some support and enthusiasm for their chosen theme of 'doof stick'! I had to rely on the fact that I have brought him up well and that he is now capable of making informed choices about certain aspects of his life. There is no way that I could have stopped him from going and honestly, nor would I have wanted to. Attending these events is like a right of passage to a young adult. I just had to trust that my child would make good decisions and that he knew I was there for him if anything went wrong. As it turned out, they all had an amazing experience and I was at least rewarded with a beautiful photo of two of my boys and their girlfriends celebrating a memorable New Years Eve together – creating memories.

The truth is, they still need us as parents, but in a different way. Therefore, as I continue to try and adapt my approach to parenting in my midlife, I've found that the most meaningful way to connect with my grown children is to show up with curiosity, not correction. Often when I ask, 'How are you feeling about that? or 'Tell me more', instead of 'Here's what I think you should do', I am invited by them to engage in a conversation. I now love the anecdotal conversations that we have as they arrive home from work and go straight to the fridge looking for food!

So as our children grow, we are also invited to grow. This chapter and stage of parenting now invites us to loosen our grip, soften our tone and trust that the time and effort that we've poured into our children during their early years is now paying dividends. It's now a time to rediscover ourselves as parents and as mothers. We're not losing our role as a Mother, we're expanding it. I am loving this opportunity to now share my wisdom, knowledge and life experiences through an open heart with my four young adult children and more so loving that they are engaging in this expanded way of parenting.

The Gift of Grandparenting

As I write this section, I haven't had the pleasure of yet becoming a grandparent. My eldest son is 23 and I know that it is still not something he and his girlfriend are planning in the next few years. My second son is 21 and he and his girlfriend are entering into the 'travel' phase of their lives which is great. The 19-year-old and his girlfriend are still navigating university and apprenticeships and my 16-year-old daughter, well that is a whole other book to be written! If I take a moment to compare parenting to what I think grandparenting will be like, I liken it to being caught in a monster wave spitting me out of its white wash and finally coming up for air compared to a stand up paddle board cruising along the gentle foreshore at Rye.

Parenting Young Adult Children and Nurturing Grandchildren

I look at the relationship between my parents and their grandchildren. I feel it's one of life's miracles that gently sneaks up on you and evokes a deeper kind of love and affection for those children. As a grandparent, I envisage a softer kind of parenting style, one that holds more patience and presence. It seems to be a love without the pressure of being the daily disciplinarian. I love watching my dad especially, sneak the chocolate or nuts or even a few dollars into their bank accounts when needed. I love the way my mum softens her tone yet still guides and educates her grandchildren. It's a special relationship that I see between grandparent and grandchild.

Grandparenting is a wonderful opportunity to have a second chance at being present for a younger human. When we are raising our own children, we were caught up in the hustle of life and most of it becomes a blur. We were busy trying to work out how to parent whilst we accommodated careers, many external responsibilities, managed expectations and all the while trying to do this through the elements of exhaustion. This all culminated in a period of life which was somewhat chaotic and we were unable to slow down. The pace with grandchildren is different. Slower. More intentional. As grandparents, we don't need to be in charge, we just get to be present and that is a rare gift.

Young adult child aged 21: 'Hey Mum, I can't wait until I have kids and you can take them to school and babysit'.

Me as parent to young adult child: 'Guess what son, I'm busy surfing that day'.

For me, I feel grandparenting isn't just about helping out when needed or being there on demand. It's about continuing the parenting of my own children and guiding them to be independent and wholesome parents themselves. I think it's healthy role modelling to show my adult children that I still have a life to live, however creating memories and being very involved in my grandchildren's lives is also going to be a priority. I want to be able to act as a memory-maker in the lives of my grandchildren. I want to share the simple ordinary moments with them such as walking on the beach, fossicking in rock pools, reading them stories, experiencing different foods and showing them a connection that is based on love, security and self-worth.

I also want to bring to light the aspect of finding your place as a grandparent in the rhythm of a new family dynamic. For me, having three boys, I am obviously not going to be the maternal grandmother and this may take a different role to that of the paternal grandmother, who knows? I am well aware that potentially, my adult children are going to parent very differently to my style of parenting. I need to be conscious of what my role as the grandparent means and how I hold that role. Perhaps only offering words of wisdom when invited might be the way to go! I need to let go of my innate tendency to instruct and control and reframe this with encouragement and support. This is how I plan on 'grandparenting with intention'.

One of the most endearing and powerful aspects that I am looking forward to through grandparenting, is that of knowing that the love I give to my children and their children is forming a part of the greater legacy that I will leave with them all. Every moment and experience I have with them, every 'hug, cuddle and whispered *I love you*', will plant a seed that will be with them for life. I see my role as a grandparent to be one that helps to raise another child to be loved, feel safe and grow into a well-rounded human that will again one day care for their children. I see grandparenting as a gift and a privilege.

Let's take a moment to stop and look towards the future or even to reflect on the space that you may be in now relating to grandparenting. Ask yourself;

Parenting Young Adult Children and Nurturing Grandchildren

In what way can I support my adult children as they parent, without taking control?

What traditions or stories from my own childhood would I love to pass on?

How do I want to role model love, kindness and curiosity for my grandchildren?

What values or life lessons do I hope my grandchildren carry with them from our relationship?

When I think about the kind of grandparent I want to be... what words come to mind?

I hope that by spending a bit of time to pause and connect with your thoughts, these questions and their answers help you to become intentional about your role as a grandparent. Happy grandparenting!

Living Your Own Life Fully

There's quite an emotional shift when that time comes whereby the house seems to empty out. I envisage that it probably happens over the space of some years, but inevitably, there may be a time where one day you are caught solid in thought, wondering where has everyone gone? The laundry pile isn't overflowing, the pantry seems to be staying fuller, the bedrooms and bathrooms are remaining clean weeks on end and there is no loud TV or music randomly blaring throughout the house. It's often classified as the 'empty nest' feeling. It's real. I tend to feel this now and again, even though I have some young adults still at home. It's a weird sense of silence that's not just the absence of noise. I can sometimes find myself sitting and suddenly missing the hustle of people in the kitchen, the need to rush to sporting practices and even the need to plan for dinner regularly. Whilst I have wished for this for a long time, when I catch myself in this moment, it can feel unexpectedly hollow and somewhat empty.

For so long, we have been someone's mum *first and foremost*. This role has shaped our days, our decisions and mostly our sense of purpose, I think. As our children now step into their own lives, we're gently reminded to ask ourselves, *'Who am I now?'* The empty nest feelings are complex and our emotions are not neatly packaged into a box. I feel there's a sense of pride as we watch our children grow and step into their adult lives through decision-making, hard work, making mistakes and fundamentally taking the lessons we have taught them into their adult world. However, alongside this sense of pride, I also feel a sense of loss. Especially with my eldest two boys who are 23 and 21, I am no longer needed in their daily lives and I do feel a tiny sense of grief; grieving the little moments, the constant presence that is no longer required and the fact that they don't necessarily tell me about absolutely everything in their lives! Not that they ever did.

There's a moment of confusion as I begin to start asking myself, *'Who am I now and what does the next phase of my life now look like?'* I want to reframe this sense of confusion, into a sense of opportunity. This phase isn't just about children growing up and leaving the nest, it's an opportunity for me to really think about the space it creates in my life and heart, and to plan and figure out how to fill it in a way that feels wholesome and joyful. In this moment as I begin to experience some of the empty nest emotions, I'm allowing them to mix together – the joy, the pride, the confusion, the excitement – in a messy layered context and tapestry, much like that of motherhood. I can feel that one enormous part of my life is not ending but transitioning and I am starting to really plan for what I want my future to look like. A future that still holds a lot of love and responsibility for my children, but the flow is in a different rhythm. I can now be the centre point and focus.

Parenting Young Adult Children and Nurturing Grandchildren

Legacy Through Love and Living By Example

Like it or not, we're on constant display to our children. For those of you who are mothers to boys, you'll probably relate to the fact that they are unique beings. I can only speak from my own experiences but coming from a family of one sister, to mothering three boys, it was a very foreign concept. I wasn't the inherent footy mum and never grasped the complex task of scoring cricket matches. I didn't want to be doing canteen duty or being the 'runner' at junior football matches. I loathed scoring the basketball and did everything in my power to avoid these parental duties. Luckily, the boys are from the same cookie cutter as their father from a sporting sense, and he took on these roles. Despite not being present at football matches or cricket matches, because let's face it, I just couldn't do it... I still play an enormous part in their lives and will undoubtedly leave a lasting legacy with all of my children. Every problem ever faced from girlfriends to boy health issues, they always did and continue to come to me for advice and support. This is where I played an important part in my boys' lives. Legacy isn't just what we leave behind in our wills or as inheritance, it's what we live out whilst we are here. Having the relationship I have with my boys (and daughter) enables my legacy to them to be seen in the warmth of my presence, my tone of voice and the way that I treat them on an individual level. That's how I want them to remember me.

The most powerful legacy that I can leave my children is the way I live my life. They are consciously and subconsciously watching their mother in her everyday activities and her life as a whole. They speak with me verbally for advice but they are also watching the way I educate myself, the way I progress in my career, what I do for relaxation, how I handle life stress and how I relate to others, just to name a few examples. They learn how I rise after setbacks, how I find joy in the things that I do and how I continue to grow and challenge myself as I enter into midlife.

The 50s Compass

Living by example is the strongest way I can leave my legacy with my children. They continue to see that as I turned 50, passion within me, particularly for surfing and taking time to enjoy my life, grew stronger. They can see that I take my health seriously and nourish my soul by taking time out of work to go to the beach and surf those waves. Here's a little anecdote of how my legacy through love and living by example is playing out:

Me as parent to young adult child: 'Hey have you got any Easter eggs left? I have literally eaten every one that is in this house and I am craving more! I really shouldn't be eating so much chocolate.'

Young adult child aged 23: 'I reckon you're ok Mum. You work out nearly every day. You're pretty healthy.'

As these words came out of his mouth, I had an overwhelming feeling of happiness and the feeling of recognition. Obviously, he's observed that I go to the gym and work hard at my weights and in his mind, I'm 'pretty healthy'. I often wonder if my children even notice all the hard work that I put in at the gym!

The greatest gift I want to offer my children is a legacy that they can too can live a fully lived life. I want them to know that I'm not perfect, but I have courage, resilience, determination, love and compassion to live my life. I feel I show up authentically for my children and this is showing them that I can follow my dreams, set boundaries when needed and show compassion and love to those around me. I don't need them to remember me for everything I have done but I do need them to remember me for authenticity and choosing a pathway that is true to oneself.

I leave you with one question – *'What do I want my life to quietly teach my children?'*

Chapter 4

Redefining Career and Purpose in Your 50s:
The Pathway to Retirement

"When I'm 50, I'll have a hundred stories, a few silver hairs, and hopefully, just as much curiosity as I do now."
— *Rapunzel, Tangled (Disney)*

"When I'm 50, I'll still be flipping patties, chasing jellyfish, and dreaming big—just with cooler glasses and maybe a few more laugh lines!" — *SpongeBob SquarePants (Disney)*

The 50s Compass

This chapter acknowledges the career achievements and education that have shaped you. This stage isn't about ceasing work or winding down, it's about repurposing and shifting a mindset towards new possibilities. You could be exploring new passions, planning for retirement or considering a career change and this chapter will embrace this transition and guide you with clarity and direction.

As I approached 50 and just after, I seemed to have different narratives swimming about in my thoughts regarding my career and work. They were a mixture of wanting to continue to climb the corporate ladder and others relating to the fact that I felt tired and really just wanted to jump in a van and head north with a surfboard on the roof. Quite contrasting thoughts and somewhat disconcerting. I have now realised that reaching your 50s does bring a surprising shift in perspectives. The career that once seemed so important and was the cornerstone to my very existence and identity, now no longer feels like such a strong driving force. I seem to now have a quiet yearning for something more fulfilling; something that fuels my soul more. To be honest, perhaps this is the driving force behind my actions of writing this book! I now feel that at the age of 50 and beyond, life is less about climbing the corporate ladder and more about climbing back into alignment with what lights me up from the inside. So, I feel like I'm not actually starting over, but I am starting wiser.

Re-purposing career and work in our 50s doesn't have to look like a grand new reinvention. It's not about starting from scratch or operationalising dreams that feel unachievable to the point where we just don't do it and continue to operate in a mindless state. I feel it's all about leveraging. Leveraging the knowledge, wisdom and experiences that we have had up until now. I feel, it's about taking time to evaluate what type of work I have been doing to this point in my life, what are my transferable skills, what do I enjoy and what flows easily. For me, I can relate to roles that involve mentoring, caring, shaping, creating and having autonomy. For those of you reading this section of my book, it may be about deciding that this is a perfect time to 'pivot' and finally use these acquired skills and knowledge to start that small business, pursue creative passions or even take up studies in a field of interest rather than a field that is defined by career progression. We are actually more equipped now in our 50s to make bold and authentic choices, not because we think we are at the end of our working careers but because our age is the catalyst for this.

As we begin to transition our career and work during midlife, interestingly it's not just our colleagues or other adults watching this change; the teenagers and young adults are too. *Interestingly, I made a flippant comment in my kitchen to my three young adult sons and their girlfriends. I said, 'Hey I just handed in my last assignment for my uni and that's the very last academic paper I plan on handing in during my lifetime'. With that comment, all eyes suddenly landed on me and they were instantly intrigued or somewhat surprised that 'I; Mum; 50-year-old; my boyfriend's mum...' had handed in a university assignment. They questioned me as to why I was doing uni at my age and what was the purpose, having thought that this was something that was only relevant to them as teenagers. So therein lay an insightful conversation during which I told them that I had done university at their age, obtained multiple degrees and Masters, worked in various settings and had now chosen to do a Graduate Certificate in Mental Health, purely out of interest and not because I had to. They seemed impressed and all gave me the teenage nod of approval before going back to consulting whatever was important on their phones!*

This glimpse into the teenage lens sparked an interest in me and remined me that our actions echo beyond our own lives. Redefining your purpose at 50 can subtly, yet profoundly, influence how the younger generation view and realise their ambitions, dreams and aspirations. I wanted to capture this for content and I wanted to know *where* these young people, particularly the girls, saw themselves when they were 50. In order to capture this content, I knew that I had to create an environment that was tech savvy to them and also didn't take up too much of their time. I promptly taught myself how to create a Google Form and I sent these out to their phones. Ironically, the girls all responded beautifully and were so engaged with this task that was asked of them.

The respondents were all female and were in the age range of 16-35 with the average age of 20 years. Through an online form, they were asked a series of open-ended questions and check lists about where they see themselves at 50. Their responses were grouped into key themes through thematic analysis and also provided some quantitative percentage data. I will point out here that although I have undertaken Masters subjects in epidemiology and statistical analysis, this is by no means an academic piece of writing! The intention here is to quench my curiosity as to where these young people saw themselves at 50 in a fun and interactive way. The respondents were chosen by me, through my own connections and I casually want to share this with you, my readers as I found it to be quite emotive and empowering (aka Girl Power). It is by no means an accurate reflection on our broader society of young women.

Theme 1: Where do I live when I'm 50?

When asked about where they saw themselves living at the age of 50, the majority of respondents answered by the ocean. This was very closely followed by living in a major city. Fifteen per cent saw themselves living overseas and the smallest percentage of respondents saw themselves as living in a small or regional town.

Theme 2: Career or Personal Fulfillment

Among respondents, whose average age was 20.4 years, many envisioned turning 50 as a milestone for achieving career goals or pursuing long-held personal passions. Over half of the group saw themselves as working in a field relating to 'helping others'. The other high ranking theme relating to career showed that they would be working in a field relating to 'creativity'. A small amount of the respondents saw themselves as working remotely or in an online environment at the age of 50. I found this section fascinating as we know that professions such as nursing and teaching are female-dominated. This was reiterated in the reponses by these girls who saw themselves in careers relating to 'helping others' when they were 50.

Theme 3: Connection and Family

When asked about their vision towards marriage, children and family at the age of 50, there was a very strong response suggesting that this group of young females saw themselves as married at the age of 50. There was also a strong tendency for this group of respondents to have an average of 3 children at the age of 50. Again, I preface that the sample size is small and that the respondents were directly approached, so this isn't a true reflection of the broader demographics in society.

Theme 4: Advice for Young Women When I'm 50

When asked what three things they would tell teenagers when they were 50, respondents shared insights that reflected their hopes for future wisdom, personal growth and life experience. There was a very strong message to not worry about what others think and to make the most of your life. Below are some anecdotes:

1. Don't stress too much it's not gonna matter in a few months time.

2. Live your life to the fullest, even if it includes making silly decisions they will be stories to tell in the future.

3. Work hard and do the things that make you happy not the things just so you can fit in.

4. Try to be yourself but also treat your parents better. They might not be right all the time, but their intentions are always good. Believe yourself that you can do everything you want to do. Treat your body better as you will be so thankful for a healthy body.

These responses paint a hopeful and inspiring picture of how young people imagine their future selves at 50. They don't see it as a time of decline, but as a time in their life of purpose, fulfillment and meaningful connection. Their visions reflect a strong desire to live with intention, stay true to their values and offer guidance to the next generation from a place of hard-earned wisdom. I feel that any perception relating to midlife as old and slowing down, is slowly shifting and I want to make sure that I'm a living example to younger women that as I live my midlife, I am sharing stories of new passions, career changes, bold travels, new relationships and connections. I want them to see midlife not as a decline but as a dynamic chapter in life filled with freedom and authenticity.

Our young ladies are hopeful for their future selves at 50 – but are you?

So, as we stand at the crossroads during midlife, it's natural to begin asking deeper questions about our career and future direction.

- *What does meaningful work look like now?*
- *Are you still energised by your current path, or is there a quiet pull toward something new?*
- *How might you repurpose your skills and passions into a role that feels more aligned with who you are today?*
- *Are you working toward retirement with intention, or simply coasting until the finish line?*

The Pathway to Retirement

These are the questions that have been swimming about in my thoughts for a while now. I've naturally found some tangible actions that have helped me to begin answering these thoughts and I've put together a guide for anyone who is feeling that quiet pull toward something more – whether it's preparing for retirement, considering a career shift, or simply craving deeper meaning in your work and life. Try some of these approaches:

Reflect Through Writing

Ask yourself

What parts of my workday energise me and really interest me?

What parts do I feel are draining or should be avoided?

If I could start over today, what would I do differently?

Take action and try to:

Set aside 10 minutes each morning or evening to journal your thoughts. Over time, patterns and truths will emerge.

Do a Skills & Passion Audit

Ask yourself

What am I naturally good at?

What do I love doing, even if I don't get paid for it?

Where do my skills and passions overlap?

Take action and try to:

Draw two overlapping circles (Venn diagram): fill one for skills and fill one for passions. In the overlapping middle section, write down the items that appear in both lists or could easily be connected. These are potential areas for aligned work, hobbies or projects. For example: Skill: Mentoring others and Passion: Personal development.

The overlap: Becoming a life coach, creating workshops, writing a self-help blog or book.

Redefine Your Version of Success

Ask yourself

What does success look like now for me using my life's acquisitions?

Is it more time, freedom, impact, creativity or peace?

Take action and try to:

Write your personal success statement: "Success for me now means using all the beautiful acquisitions in my life in a way that brings happiness, fulfillment and leaves space for rest and restoration".

Try Before You Leap

Ask yourself

What's one small way I can explore this interest or new direction?

Can I take a course, volunteer or start a side project?

Take action and try to:

Commit to trying one new thing in the next 30 days. It doesn't have to be big – just a step.

Reimagine Retirement

Ask yourself

What would it look like to retire into an environment that excites me?

How do I want to feel in this next chapter of life?

Take action and try to:

Start building a vision board or list what you'd like retirement to include – passions, people, places and projects.

Seek Out Mentors or Coaches

Ask yourself

Who do I admire who has made a midlife shift?

What could I learn from someone who's walked this path?

Take action and try to:

Reach out to one person in your network who's made a change in midlife. Consider working with a coach to help shape your direction. This could be the catalyst you are looking for and well worth the investment.

Final Thoughts

You don't have to have all the answers now. You just need the courage to ask better questions – and take one intentional step at a time.

So, whether you're planning for retirement, exploring new passions or considering a career change, this transition doesn't have to be marked by uncertainty. It's really an invitation. Repurposing your energy and experience at this stage of life means recognising that wisdom, resilience and curiosity are powerful tools for growth. I absolutely embrace this phase and focus on not starting over; but moving forward with a clearer purpose and a renewed sense of self. Exciting!

Chapter 5

Reflecting on Relationships and Connections:
Who Are Your People?

This is a powerful time to reflect on the relationships that matter the most. This chapter will help you identify who your 'people' are – those who truly understand, uplift and encourage and understand and challenge you. It's a time to declutter your relationships and connections and let go of what no longer serves you. This allows time to focus on what brings joy and upholds your values so that you can continue fostering positive connections that enrich the next part of your life.

The 50s Compass

The famous quote from the 1937 Disney film, *Snow White and the Seven Dwarfs* is:

"Magic mirror on the wall, who is the fairest one of all?"

The Midlife Mirror

Often at this point in our lives, if we take a moment to stand in front of the mirror and take a long look at not only the person standing in the reflection, but a deeper look into what's inside, we find that there is a profound array of turbulence brewing. We are still juggling careers, raising and hoping to release our children into adulthood, managing households, caring for ageing parents and perhaps even navigating divorce or trying to reimagine romantic lives. As we look in the mirror and amidst all of these moving parts in life, one quiet but often powerful question to ask ourselves is: *Who are my people?*

If I think back the people in my life at the age of 20, 30 and even 40, there is a shift. The relationships that once defined my sense of belonging have shifted and even faded. Childhood and school friends who were once such a poignant part of my construct and almost defined who I was, are now a distant memory. Work colleagues are important to me but those relationships walk a fine line between professional and personal and more often, should not extend beyond the job boundary. Interestingly, some family relationships of mine have also strained and shifted in dynamic. A very real contrast to the dynamic that was occurring when I was much younger. Yet, in this exact phase of my life, there has been a quiet emergence of new women in my life. These women have and continue to give me new depth, perspective and unexpected support from surprising places. They have entered mainly through my surfing connections but also through different avenues as I am pursuing my passions and writing this book is a prime example. I've thoroughly come to the realisation that I have more power than ever to choose who gets my energy.

This chapter acts as a mirror. It's an invitation to look deeply and gently examine your connections.

- Which ones nourish you?
- Which ones no longer fit with you?
- How do you cultivate a circle that supports the woman or person you are becoming?

Navigating the Shifts

By the time we reach 50-something, many of our roles and relationships have undertaken immense shifts. We may no longer identify solely as someone's mother, wife, partner or colleague. There have been so many events that have occurred to land us in this position. We now enter into midlife and may subconsciously or consciously ask: *Who am I when I'm not needed by someone else?*

Naturally as we grow and change, so too do our relationships and connections (or they may not). Sometimes we may hold on too long, feeling guilty for outgrowing someone who once meant so much. Growth, however, doesn't mean loss; it means making room for what's aligned with your present self and direction. It's interesting to take a moment to ask yourself: Who in my life has grown with me? Who holds space for me as my authentic self now?

The Role of Intimate Relationships

Divorce in midlife can feel like a landslide or a tidal wave. The event that you are not prepared for, that there is no instruction manual for and that there is no cookie cutter/one shoe fits all approach.

The 50s Compass

It's an event that can shake your identity, redefine your family construct and absolutely challenge your sense of safety. But it can also be a redefining moment and set a clear path for rediscovery.

Whether you initiated the ending or not, divorce or the ending of a long-term relationship is fraught with grief and sadness, yet also eventually offers an invitation to come home to yourself. Once the dust has settled – and this may take years – there awaits an invitation to reimagine what love, independence and joy can look and feel like. For some of us, that may mean a return to being single with newfound confidence. A chance to realign and reassess who we want as long-term partners, if any. It may also mean co-parenting with flexibility and respect or exploring the construct of blended families.

On a personal note, this is a sensitive and challenging topic to write about. I don't resonate with the term, 'happily divorced'. In my mind, we don't get married to get divorced. I am amicably divorced and have a very healthy and respectful relationship with my ex-husband. Hey, we often run into each other at the gym and poke fun at each other as he asks me to spot him on the weights! We live close by and our children interchangeably go across houses. Divorce for me was both a deeply challenging and liberating experience. It absolutely came with emotional pain, financial complications and the upheaval of our long-established routines and family dynamics. It did bring a sense of loss, identity confusion and fear about starting over. Yet on the other hand, it also served as a powerful reset. It offered me the opportunity to reconnect with my individuality, realign with my values and build a life that feels authentic and fulfilling. Five years on, I have found new strength, clarity, and purpose in the aftermath of a 20-year marriage. I'm discovering that it's never too late to redefine what love, happiness and self-worth can look like. There's a strong affirmation that I hold close: *I am allowed to redefine what partnership means for me.*

Who Are Your People?

Romance After 50

As I begin to write this section, I've actually taken a moment to pause and a small smirk has emerged from within. How do I approach this section? There are so many roads that I could take it down. I am having a chuckle to myself because something that someone said to me always sticks in my mind:

Dating after 40 is like looking through a used car yard and trying to find the least broken one...

Dating in midlife is like shopping at a used car yard or rummaging through an op shop – you're not always sure what you'll find, but there's definitely character, history and the occasional pleasant delight. The dating apps feel like a weird game show whereby it's a tick or flick and everyone is trying to tell their story in five photos and a catchy, cringe worthy tagline ("Best catch ever, catch of the day"). You might need to sharpen your skills in perception and listening to your inner voice just to spot and dodge the red flags, and let's be honest, there's a few of them flying from everyone's emotional baggage compartment. But amongst the awkward coffee dates and overused emojis from a generation who really has no idea how to use them, there's a potentially refreshing honesty that comes with age and life experience. That is, no time for games, just real conversations, good laughs and the possibility of surprising new connections when you least expect it. Now I know that is absolutely writing this section from a glass half full perspective, but I feel that there needs to be a sense of humour and light-heartedness captured in this.

In this chapter of your fairytale, the happily-ever-after doesn't begin with or depend upon a prince charming or a perfect match – it starts with you. Midlife dating must, must, must become less about *being* chosen and more about choosing yourself: romancing your own heart, honouring your own values and embracing the life you've built with grace and hard work. You now become both the heroine and the author in this next fairytale chapter, rewriting the rules and wearing that princess crown on your own terms. Whether love arrives in the form of a new partner or blossoms from within, this is your enchanted moment to dance across the grounds of the castle you've created, knowing that the most powerful love story is the one where you never stop choosing yourself.

I'm a true romantic at heart and as a Libran, I am ruled by the planet Venus. Venus is strongly associated with love, beauty, balance and we are inclined towards social connections, artistic passions and have a very strong focus on relationships. Therefore, I can't finish this section without providing some practical tips for building a love story for yourself!

Practical Tips for Creating Your Own Midlife Love Story

♥ Date Yourself First

Schedule regular solo dates that bring you pleasure and joy – whether it's a quiet walk, a favourite café or even just dancing in your living room. This builds self-trust and reinforces that your own company is enough – it's so uplifting.

♥ Revisit (or Rewrite) Your Values

Ask yourself: What matters most to me now? Write down your top 5 core values. Let these guide both your relationships and how you show up for yourself. These are your 'True North'.

♥ Celebrate Your Desires Without Shame

Do you want companionship? Passion? Freedom? All of it? Own your desires unapologetically. They're not selfish – they're signals

Who Are Your People?

pointing you toward what makes life rich and meaningful. It's very liberating.

💜 Create Rituals of Self-Romance

Light candles, wear the perfume, use the good wine glasses and feel into that feminine energy. Romance doesn't need an audience or to be advertised – it's a mindset of making life feel delicious and sacred, just for you.

💜 Set Clear Love Standards

Know the difference between a fantasy and your needs. Define your non-negotiables in a partner (if dating), or in how you want to feel in any relationship, including the one with yourself. If dating, don't prolong any red flags. Set your standards and intentions and cut it off quickly if those red flags immerge.

💜 Be the Heroine of Your Narrative

Stop waiting for a magical rescue or the knight in shining armour. You're the author of this fairytale. What does your version of happily-ever-after look like now? Begin living it – not someday, but today.

I'm hoping that now during midlife, you realise that the castle's been yours all along, the princess tiara fits just fine and the real fairytale is the one where you fall madly and deeply in love... with yourself. You light your own candles, buy your own flowers and know that a well-seasoned woman with strong values and a good set of life experiences is a force to be reckoned with. Whether Prince Charming shows up or not, you're already writing a love story for the future and for your legacy – one filled with laughter, freedom, self-worth and the kind of joy that doesn't need rescuing. In the words of Miley Cyrus in her song Flowers;

The 50s Compass

I can buy myself flowers

Write my name in the sand

Talk to myself for hours

Say things you don't understand

I can take myself dancing

And I can hold my own hand

Yeah, I can love me better than you can

Caring for Ageing Parents

Somewhat like the phase of empty nesting creeps up slowly, so too does the role of caring for ageing parents. The experience of becoming caregivers to our parents may arrive suddenly during midlife. There may be the increasing requirement to accompany them to medical appointments, assist with scheduling these, communicating and interacting with them as they begin to experience a decline in their physical abilities, all the while doing this with gentle support and not overstepping into their independence.

It's a tender and perhaps tedious transition that can stir up old family wounds or bring unexpected closeness within family relationships. It can be a tedious transition as we are still balancing work, children and our own challenging needs. This is a period that really calls for both emotional resilience and practical planning, as roles shift and we become the carer to our parents. As well as managing their medical appointments, we may have to begin making collaborative financial decisions in addition to acknowledging and managing the emotional weight of watching a once-independent parent become more vulnerable. As a registered nurse and having worked in the health sector my whole life, I feel it's essential to communicate openly with siblings, access community resources and set realistic boundaries to avoid burnout. I definitely believe that when caring for ageing parents the old mantra of *'failing to plan is planning to fail'*. While this chapter can be heavy, it also offers moments of tenderness, connection and even healing – opportunities to honour your parents' journey while re-evaluating your own values around aging, support and legacy. Amid the demands, don't forget to care for yourself too because you can't pour from an empty cup, especially when you're supporting the generation before you.

As mentioned before, I've nursed in aged care, worked in State Government overseeing aged care policies and also worked in a large tertiary hospital assisting vulnerable community to navigate the aged care system – all of which is complex and daunting. Here are some helpful strategies that can make this inevitable process just a little easier:

Practical Tips for Caring for Ageing Parents in Midlife

👤 Start the Conversation Early

Don't wait for a crisis or an emergency to take place. Talk with your parents about their wishes for medical care, living arrangements, finances and end-of-life preferences while they're still able to clearly express them. They should be investing time in formulating their advanced care planning process with the health care provider.

👤 Get the Legal Essentials in Order

Ensure all the key documents are in place and clearly understood: Power of Attorney (medical & financial), Advanced Care Plan, Will and access to important account information (banking, insurance, healthcare) is all in place. It's also advisable to consult a lawyer or elder care advisor if needed.

👤 Create a Care Team

You don't have to do it all single-handed. Involve siblings, trusted friends, neighbours or professionals. Delegate tasks such as transport, grocery shopping or life administration and consider rotating care if possible.

👤 Use Community & Government Resources

Tap into and learn about aged care programs, home support services, respite care and meal delivery. In Australia, start with My Aged Care (myagedcare.gov.au) for assessments and access to subsidised services. There are many supports in place to assist.

👤 Set Boundaries Without Guilt

This is important for everyone's wellbeing, and it's important to remember that you can be loving and still say no. Prioritise your own mental and physical health because burnout helps no one. Schedule breaks, say yes when you can and ask for help when you need it.

👤 Keep a Medical & Appointment Log

Track medications, health conditions, appointments and relevant paperwork in one place. Apps like Medisafe Pill Reminder or a shared Google Docs can help coordinate between family members and ensure that everyone has oversight to the day to day needs.

Who Are Your People?

👤 Stay Patient: But Realistic

Be mindful that ageing can bring behaviour changes, memory loss, mood shifts or resistance to help. Approach your parents with empathy but stay firm when safety is at stake. Sometimes being the 'bad guy' means protecting them.

👤 Make Time for Connection

This is a time to sometimes just create a space for meaningful moments beyond the hustle of everyday life. Sit and have that cup of tea and share stories, look through old photos, cook a meal together – small but thoughtful rituals preserve dignity and enjoyment for all involved.

As I write this, I reflect on my own situation. I vividly remember going to Zumba classes with my beautiful father who was aged 70 at the time and celebrated this by being brought up onto the Zumba stage to dance. I have the best photo of this and can vividly see the smile and happiness on his face when he did this. I fast forward now 10 years, and whilst he is still completely mobile and actively playing golf and travelling, I know that I will never have the chance to share a laughter-filled Zumba class with him again. Caring for ageing parents is one of the most profound acts of love and reciprocity we'll ever offer to them. It's a full-circle moment where we (their children), become the steady hand and guide they once were for us. It's not always easy and I envisage it to be messy, exhausting and emotionally draining. But within the challenges of this phase lies something sacred; the chance to honour their journey, preserve their dignity and hold space for the shared memories that shaped us as a family unit. As the Dalai Lama wisely said, *"Be kind whenever possible. It is always possible."*

Friendships and Connections that Nourish

Midlife is a time to stop and re-evaluate friendships and connections. Some relationships that have stood the test of time might now feel strained or shallow and newly formed ones may become lifelines, there to the very end. Friendships and connections take on a new kind of richness in this phase of life. I feel they're no longer about quantity or convenience, but more about depth, alignment and mutual nourishment. The casual friendships I had in my twenties may have faded, the particular cliques no longer serve me, and even some long-standing bonds have shifted as I've grown into fuller versions of myself. But midlife also presents the opportunity to form new connections that reflect who we are now and not who we used to be.

The Friends Who Feed Your Soul

True friendship in midlife isn't measured in daily texts or coffee catch-ups but in emotional safety and laughter that lights you up coupled with the ease of being authentically yourself when in their presence. These are the friends who ask how you really are and wait for the answer. The ones who support your growth, cheer your wins and hold space during your messier chapters in life during which they hear the same story over and over again. Nourishing friendships aren't always loud or prominent all over the social media posts – they're often quiet, steady and fiercely loyal.

If your friendship circle has changed or feels smaller – know that this is normal. Life chapters close, priorities evolve and as we become more intentional and considerate with our time and energy, our friendships naturally refine. Letting go of friendships that no longer align can be painful, but it makes room for more life-giving connections to enter.

Who Are Your People?

Colleagues Turned Kindreds

In midlife, our working relationships also take on more significance. We spend a huge portion of our time with our colleagues and while some connections remain purely professional, others develop into genuine friendships. These are the people who understand the daily grind, who share your wins and who may even challenge you to grow. Nurturing positive work connections can make your professional life more fulfilling and reduce burnout during the later stage in our careers.

If you're shifting careers or planning a transition, your professional network can also become a valuable support system. Don't hesitate to reach out, reconnect or build new ones. Sometimes the people who can help you take your next leap are already around you – you just need to ask. Writing this book is a prime example of how I have taken a leap of faith out of my world in healthcare and made new friendships within the writing scene. It's so new but so rewarding.

Professional and Emotional Support

Friendship isn't the only kind of connection that nourishes in midlife. This is also the time to lean into professional and therapeutic support systems. A coach, mentor, therapist, or women's group can offer clarity, reflection and tools to navigate the big questions that often arise in this season: Who am I now? What do I want next? How do I build the courage to go after it?

Investing in these relationships isn't a sign of weakness – it's a declaration of self-worth and boy do we deserve it by this stage. Whether it's guidance on navigating empty nesting, career change, menopause or grief, having a professional mentor around you can be transformative. I have engaged with a professional mentor over a 12-month period and this has enabled me to answer some pretty heavy questions that will determine my true north. I don't think I would have been able to establish the root cause of some of my decision making and her guidance has enabled me to do this.

Creating New Connections

It's never too late to find your people. You might meet them at a book club, a yoga class, an online forum or a volunteer role. Be open to the unexpected because sometimes kindred spirits appear in unlikely places. If you feel disconnected, try stepping gently outside your comfort zone. Say yes to an invitation. Reach out to someone you've been meaning to get to know. Let curiosity lead the way. I set myself up with a goal for a 12-month period under the banner of – Reconnecting. This meant, that for 12 months I had to intentionally reconnect or make new connections with people outside my comfort zone. It has led me into circles that I never envisaged I would be in. I cannot be more grateful.

Checking-In with Your Circle

Take a moment now to reflect on these questions:

- ✿ Who brings you energy, and who drains it?
- ✿ Who do you feel safe to be your full self with?
- ✿ Is there someone you miss and want to reconnect with?
- ✿ Are there people you're holding onto out of obligation rather than mutual nourishment?

Honouring your need for meaningful connection means trusting your gut and choosing relationships that feel mutual, kind and growth-oriented.

Who Are Your People?

Closing Thoughts

Midlife is not about shrinking your world – it's about enriching it and one of the most powerful ways to do that is through the people you surround yourself with. Choose relationships that make you feel warm, real and life-affirming. Let go of what no longer serves. Be brave enough to reach out. Always, always leave space in your circle for both new faces and the ones who've stayed by your side.

> **"You are the average of the five people you spend the most time with." – Jim Rohn**

Jim Rohn, a well-known motivational speaker and entrepreneur, used this phrase to highlight the powerful influence that our inner circle has on our mindset, habits and overall success. I use it in my personal life and professional life to reflect on relationships and to be intentional about surrounding myself with supportive, inspiring and growth-minded individuals.

Try this:

Create yourself a 'relationship map'. Put your name in the centre of a piece of paper. The write the names of people in your life, positioning them according to the closeness and connection that they have with you.

- ❋ Who is in your inner circle?
- ❋ Who might you gently move the outer edges?
- ❋ Who are you calling in?

You get to design and monitor this map because you have the ability and creativity to do so.

The 50s Compass

Chapter 6

The Exciting Road Ahead:
Setting Intentions for an Inspiring and Fulfilling Next Chapter

Who remembers in primary school when we were asked to write either a fable, story or poem that had a specific moral or lesson in it? You were probably sitting cross-legged on the floor mat staring whimsically up at the teacher with a puzzled look on your face. I remember I chose to write about how the toucan got its beak and the moral of the story was that this bird needed a special beak in order to look regal and important in the jungle to stand out from the bird crowd! So, in honour of this task that I can remember so clearly, I've cleared the cobwebs from my brain and have taken myself back to Mr Men days. Here's my attempt at a playful, heartwarming Mr. Men and Little Miss-style story designed to reflect the theme of living your best life in midlife.

Mr Mojo & Little Miss Midlife

A Tale of Living Your Best Life (Even When You Think You're Too Old)

Mr Mojo had once been very groovy. Back in his twenties, he danced under the strobe lights at night clubs and occasionally found himself up on the podiums, rode his BMX bike around especially to the milkbar for sneaky cigarettes and woke up without groaning every time he bent over to pick his clothes up off the floor. But now, Mr Mojo was in his 50s and lately, he felt… well, a little meh. His glittery shirts and tight jeans were stuffed in a drawer. His new Nike 270 gym shoes had barely been worn. He even skipped the annual Blues Fest held in Byron Bay (a clear sign that something was off).

"I think I've lost my spark and my mojo," he sighed one morning, staring into his well-separated protein shake.

Enter: Little Miss Midlife – his fabulously grounded friend who wore nice fitting colour coordinated active wear and always carried a notebook of dreams.

"Oh, Mr Mojo," she grinned. "You didn't lose your spark or your mojo. You've just forgotten where you've left it."

She handed him her notebook of dreams and showed him a list titled 'Living Your Best Life, Starting Now'.

It read:

- ❀ Try something new every month, even if it's just a new flavour of tea or food.

Setting Intentions for an Inspiring and Fulfilling Next Chapter

- ✿ Move your body like it loves you (not like you're punishing it).
- ✿ Ditch what drains you. Turn up what lights you up.
- ✿ Laugh. A lot. Even in the mirror and especially at your own dad jokes.
- ✿ Dream like you're 25, but plan like you're 55.
- ✿ Wear the glitter shirt. Life's too short for beige.

Mr Mojo stared at the list that was in front of him. He began to laugh but he also cried a little. He realised that he still had that younger Mr Mojo inside him, however he'd been shut down and put to the back of the closet for quite some time. This made him sad.

Over the next few weeks, Mr Mojo took some time to really think about what he wanted from now on. He knew that he could continue to feel 'meh' and probably that was the easiest option as it required not much effort. However, after reminiscing about the times when he did feel alive and totally fulfilled, he decided to take some of the advice from Little Miss Midlife's notebook. He dug out the glitter shirt and put it on, albeit tight! He put on some funky disco music that he used to listen to in the clubs (a bit of The Only Way is Up by Yaz) and started dancing around his room. He looked in the mirror and laughed at himself. Mr Mojo was feeling more energised now and he decided to join a bike club through the community Facebook page. He loved being outside with other like-minded people. Once a week, he and Little Miss Midlife would meet up to share their latest 'little life upgrades' over a coffee and cake.

Eventually, Mr. Mojo realised: living his best life wasn't about going backwards. It was about leaning joyfully into now. His body may feel a bit less flexible and his knees may protest after a night of dancing, but his inner soul? It's still ready to boogie.

And so, Mr Mojo found his spark again. Right where he left it – in the middle of living.

The 50s Compass

The Moral:

You're never too old to rediscover happiness, chase meaning or rock a glitter shirt. Midlife isn't a slowdown, **it's a glow-up**.

This is the optimal time to embrace the opportunity to shape the road ahead. This chapter will inspire you to look towards your true north with excitement, not just for the future but for the power that you have to create it. It's about exploring fresh possibilities, setting new goals and directions and stepping into midlife with a youthful pep in your step. The road ahead is yours to design, filled with limitless potential for happiness, creativity and connectedness; live the life you've always imagined.

By the time you have come to this section in my book, we all agree that midlife is not a pause; **it's a powerful pivot**. It's a point on the map where the road behind you offers wisdom and the road ahead is yours to shape with clarity, courage and intention. While those around us may continue to paint this stage with tired clichés of slowing down and heading towards the end of our lives... we know that the truth is far more inspiring: **midlife is a rebirth**. It's a time to reconnect with your deepest values, reimagine your future and recalibrate how you live, love and lead.

Become the Living Midlife Example

Setting intentions for your next chapter is about more than just goal-setting. It's about consciously aligning your energy – emotionally, mentally and physically – with what lights you up and brings meaning to your days. You don't need a total reinvention.

Setting Intentions for an Inspiring and Fulfilling Next Chapter

You just need to listen inward, clear some space and boldly begin where you are.

All throughout this book I've spoken to key themes about emotional, mental and physical connections and alignment. By combining these three fundamental elements, you are going to enable your true alignment and an unbreakable connection to your intentions and ultimate goals. So, I want to finish this book with a culmination of bringing all of this together with you so that you become the living example of your life.

Emotional Wellbeing: Honouring Your Inner Landscape

We are emotionally filled beings and your emotional life in midlife deserves attention and nourishment. We are able to express our emotions verbally and that is what sets us apart from all other creatures. At this point in life, we have weathered decades of joy, heartbreak, love and loss and every emotion has helped shaped our resilience. The emotional connection that we have to something is the foundation of our reasoning for why we want to achieve a certain goal and now is the time to tune into what you feel instead of what you're supposed to feel. Setting intentions here means asking: What do I want more of emotionally? What do I need to let go of?

Step 1 – Determine how you want to feel
Before setting the goal, work out how you want to feel. Then ask yourself, 'Will this goal or intention generate this feeling?' If it won't, then it's not right for you. The emotional connection must be right as it can manifest many subsequent goals and outcomes in the future. It is the missing link and the element that can have the greatest impact. Just imagine, if you could feel this driving emotion (whether it is satisfaction, calmness or determination) every day... imagine the influence it would have on your mindset.

Imagine the impact it would have on the momentum that you bring into your life. Your emotion is the fuel that will propel you towards your goals sooner.

Step 2 – Be inspiring
In order to be inspiring, you firstly need to be inspired. Often by midlife, we are a bit tired and take on a 'ho hum' approach. You need to consciously put yourself in inspiring environments and challenge yourself to find ways to recharge your energy, your passion and your soul. We all know that life and people can wear us down and so much so that it is vital that you immerse yourself into inspiring environments. I have taken my own advice here and immersed myself into a world of new first-time authors and the connections and stories I have experienced are so inspiring! If you are inspired, you will automatically become a living example for those around you and perhaps for people whom you have never met.

Step 3 – Intentional actions
I ask that you take some action towards honouring your inner landscape and tapping into those positive emotions that are going to propel you through midlife.

- ✿ Start a daily 'emotional check-in' practice to name and validate your feelings.
- ✿ Cultivate relationships that feel emotionally reciprocal and safe.
- ✿ Consider a therapist, coach or support group to explore unresolved emotional patterns.

Mental Clarity: Reframing Your Thoughts and Expanding Possibility

Midlife often brings a shift in mental focus as we move from the focus of proving ourselves to understanding ourselves. Mental

Setting Intentions for an Inspiring and Fulfilling Next Chapter

power is about having resilience that can take us into a new chapter. We need our mental power to cleanse and declutter outdated beliefs, silence the inner critic and make space for new perspectives. Mental intention-setting is about rewiring the story you tell yourself. Are your thoughts empowering or limiting? Are you holding onto narratives that no longer serve the person you're becoming?

Step 1: Change your language
The words that you use everyday make a difference. If you want to enhance your mental power, then change the way you speak to yourself. It's essential that you move your language patterns and internal dialogue from; 'I will try' to 'I will do'; from 'I think' to 'I believe'; from 'some day' to 'when', from 'could' to 'can' and from 'how' to 'why'. My prime example is – How can I write a book? This was reframed to, 'Why do I want to write a book?' Can you see that the second phrase is backed and fuelled by emotional intent? This relates right back to Chapter 1 where I talk about discovering your WHY and your passion.

Step 2: Stop worrying
There's a great quote by the German born self-help author, Eckhart Tolle. He's best know for his book, The Power of Now. With respect to worrying, Tolle says,

> "Worry pretends to be necessary but
> serves no useful purpose."

This is also a beautiful time to nourish your curiosity and your intellect and to let go of what other people think, as really, it's none of their business. Let go of worry and don't seek approval from anyone else because the only approval you need is your own. Rather than focussing on a worrying thought, channel your energy into taking meaningful actions and celebrate the fact that you are moving in a positive direction.

The 50s Compass

Step 3: Be happy
There's a common narrative that goes on in our heads – 'as soon as the kids are older', 'as soon as I buy the new car,' 'as soon as I retire', 'as soon as I have enough money' and 'as soon as I lose weight'...

We've all said it and we all probably continue to say it! These words are a combination of procrastination and also wanting more and not being happy in the present time. There are some wise words spoken by the well known Greek philosopher, Socrates, who was known for his profound insights on wisdom, knowledge and the human experience:

'He who is not content with what he has would not be content with what he would like to have.'

Socrates was philosophising that true satisfaction comes from within and not from external circumstances or material possessions. Therefore, if someone can't find peace or satisfaction in their current situation, acquiring more wealth, status or possessions won't magically make them happier. The desire for more can become endless if it's driven by inner dissatisfaction. This quote suggests that fulfillment is a mindset and not a milestone. If we learn to appreciate the present and foster gratitude, then this is the key to lasting happiness, rather than constantly chasing after the next thing.

Similarly, by putting off actions, procrastination can offer a temporary relief but it often takes away the momentum and joy that is found in the present moment. If we are constantly holding off and because the narrative in our heads is a future promise of 'as soon as...', we risk missing the beautiful opportunities that exist only in the here and now. Life evolves in real time, not in the past or in distant plans – it's occurring now! So if you choose to act rather then postpone or wish for more before you act, you can align yourself with growth, presence and determined purpose.

Setting Intentions for an Inspiring and Fulfilling Next Chapter

Living in the present moment means embracing each moment as it happens and offers a chance to create, connect and move forward rather than letting these opportunities pass by weighted down with hesitation and fear.

My advice is to start now from where you stand, start now and take action quickly. It doesn't have to be big, just a small step.

It was a Sunday morning and I was lying in bed aimlessly scrolling through my phone (as we all do). I came across a post that made me stop and read. It was the topic that grabbed my attention. I saw the words 'First Time Author'. Now intrinsically we all have passions and interests that lie dormant, and writing is one of these for me. I have written countless academic papers and policy papers, which weirdly, I really enjoy doing. However, these obviously lack the creative edge and freedom for me. So I think that's why this post that was relating to being a first-time author really took my eye.

Suddenly my emotions were heightened and I felt a small sense of excitement transverse through me. I had a fleeting thought, that maybe I could be a first-time author and write a book. Driven by this emotion, I stopped scrolling and read through the post. A lot of the wording was completely foreign to me. It talked about manuscripts, publishing, content creation and digital marketing. I was from a world of health and government and these were terms that I hadn't been immersed in. I felt uncomfortable and nearly decided to keep scrolling. However, the emotion of excitement and freedom was now alive and I read on to see that there was a free seminar being held in Melbourne. I thought for a moment and then enacted all the words of wisdom that I've imparted in this book for you and – clicked register and attend!

Fast forward to the day of the seminar, and I did go. To be honest, it felt really strange going to a seminar that wasn't in my industry field with people I knew nothing about. I turned up to the front door and was given a name badge that said; Sarah (Author). What? Why was the word 'author' next to my name? I very quickly felt out of my depth and slowly found my way to back section of the room. I was even more intimidated when I started to speak to people around me who were talking about how they were writing their memoirs, writing about their experiences working in the fields of mental health, armed forces, there were people who were doctors and psychologists writing about their field of expertise. The one author who suddenly made me feel at ease was one who was selling her published book at this event and it was focussed on her experiences of being a midwife. Now I began to feel more comfortable and I actually bought a copy of her book before the seminar started.

My point to this story, is that there is merit in starting now from where you stand, starting now and starting quickly. If I hadn't quickly taken action and pressed the registration button to this free seminar, I would not be here today writing my first book. I had absolutely no knowledge of the world of writing, except for the fact that I love doing it. I think this journey that I am on is a prime example of not waiting until I was good enough, until the kids finished school, until I had more time or until I retired. I bit the bullet so to speak and look where I am now.

Step 4: Pay the price

Here I am not talking about the dollars you pay. Action is the price you need to pay in order to achieve your goals and fulfillment. What price are you willing to pay to pursue your passions? This doesn't need to be in dollar amounts, but in time and energy. Another way to look at this is, how much is it costing you by *not* doing what you love? What mindset are you in, what example are you setting, what messages are you sending out to others and what habits are you forming by not taking action?

No matter what, we will always pay a price in time, money and energy. Therefore, we want a good return on investment so making

Setting Intentions for an Inspiring and Fulfilling Next Chapter

sure we act now in some small way is so important. It costs nothing to dream big. Make a decision, move forward and if it's not the right decision, make another one. Make progress and continue to move forward as you pursue your passion.

Afterword

Writing the Next Chapter with Intention

It's vital to set an intenion because then you point your internal compass towards what matters most. This intenion isn't about designing rigid goals or seeking external validation from friends and family; it's about deliberately choosing how you want to feel, live and experience this vibrant next chapter.

The 50s Compass

What kind of woman am I becoming?

What do I want more of in my life every single day?

What legacy do I want to leave behind personally, professionally and emotionally?

For a short summary and some take home non-negotiables of what to do next to create the fullest life, to do what matters, what makes a difference and to become the best living version of yourself, here are the **10 Non-Negotiables of Now**.

This is your midlife roadmap. The top ten constant commitments that will continue to move you forward with clarity, courage, and emotional intent.

1. Listen to your inner voice
    - ✿ Reconnect with your truth
2. Move with purpose
    - ✿ Move your body to celebrate it
3. Protect your energy
    - ✿ Say no to what drains you
4. Craft your circle
    - ✿ Connect with those who reflect yourself
5. Do what matters first
    - ✿ Don't let urgency overpower importance
6. Look in the mirror and get real with yourself
    - ✿ Be brave enough to face the areas where you're stuck
7. Practice daily gratitude
    - ✿ Shift your thinking from deficits to abundance
8. Live with brave dreams
    - ✿ Imagine boldly and don't shrink your dreams
9. Don't be a bystander
    - ✿ Contribute actively to your world

Writing the Next Chapter with Intention

10. Choose yourself everyday
    - ✿ Show up for yourself consistently and courageously

Thank you for taking the time to read my first ever book. It has been a culmination of stories, interests and pearls of wisdom that I have collected over the course of my life until now; midlife. I hope that you have taken something away with you that is going to propel you into the next phase. I also hope that this book has given you the energy and intent not to phase out but to rise and shine. May all your incredible dreams come alive while you continue to pursue and chase your passion and live a life that you truly deserve.

Epilogue

As I conclude the writing of my first book, I do so with a sense of accomplishment. It was a pipeline dream to write a book and to be able to share my adventures with others in the hope that I would be able to inspire those around me. I would like to finish my book through a letter to my dear friend and soulmate; Richard.

Dear Richard,

Even though you have left this world and have left me to take on midlife without you, I just want you to know that things are going well. Your presence continues to linger with me like a soft echo as I often hear your voice in my ears. I hear you when I am feeling stuck or like I can't move forward. I hear you say, 'Just get on with it, don't give up, push through'.

There are often times when I've ridden a beautiful wave and trimmed the line so well, that I finish and look to the beach to see if you are

The 50s Compass

watching. I'm looking for you to give me that nod of approval or the thumbs up indicating that I've done well. Of course, you aren't there and it's in that split second that I realise, I just have to be proud of myself from within. I've learnt now that I don't need external recognition or approval to do what I do.

I've taken the lessons that you've taught me and continue to live through my passions. You told me to have that one thing that truly lights me up and gets me out of bed in the morning, the one thing I think about when I am working yearning for the weekend. Of course, that is being in the ocean and surfing. You'll be pleased to know that since you have left this earth, I have continued to join new surfing groups, go on different surf trips and commit to surfing as often as I can. You'll even be surprised that I did a free diving course but chickened out at the 10m boat dive as I didn't want to fail equalising my ears and blow an ear drum!

Remember how you supported me through my divorce and were so tolerant of my fluctuating and crazy emotions? Remember I used to call you often, crying uncontrollably and constantly wanting hugs and reassurance? I remember your words of support and the calm way in which you guided me through this unknown territory. You told me to concentrate on myself and to provide a safe and secure environment for my kids. Well, I'm pleased to say that I've weathered that storm and have come out the other end. I love my house, I love where I live and I love the fact that my growing teenage children are all finished and finishing school and entering into their next phase of adulthood and work. Even 'daughter' is doing so well in Year 11. You would be proud of her.

Speaking of kids, before I sign off and say a final goodbye, I want to let you know that your boy, Will, is doing so well. He's 21 now and he and I continue to share such a wonderful unique bond. You know, when I am missing you and thinking of you, randomly, Will will reach out and call me. Just the other night, I was missing you

Epilogue

terribly, and scrolling through Facebook looking at diving scenes on the Great Barrier Reef. I thought, in that instant, I should text Will, and with that he called me. It's unexplainable. Remember how we would argue about the fact that you wanted him to join the Navy and he was adamant that he didn't want to? Well, I want you to know that he has successfully finished his time on Hamilton Island chartering the ferries and now he is a private Skipper on a yacht based out of a marina near Brisbane. You would be so proud.

So, I guess in writing this book, which I started with a personal anecdote about our 'love story', I now find myself at the end, circling back. I think back on our relationship and all the antics and adventures we got up to as young adults. Now in midlife, I'm reminded that it's never really too late to listen to my life. To choose again and reconnect with meaningful intentions. So, as you look down from above, know that I do miss you so much but you have given me that nudge I needed to stay true to my own path.

You are forever in my heart and thoughts,

Sarah xx

About the Author

Sarah was born and raised on Wurundjeri Country (Melbourne, Australia) and is the eldest daughter to two migrant parents. Her father was born in Penang, Malaysia and her mother was born in Glasgow, Scotland. She is the proud mother to four children, who continuously manage to make her laugh and smile. She loves watching her three sons grow into independent and emotionally sensitive men and her daughter navigate her role as the youngest child with three older brothers.

Sarah has had a diverse and fulfilling professional career. She has worked for many years as a neonatal intensive care nurse which was a significant and rewarding part of her working life. She feels extremely fortunate and holds immense gratitude to each of the families who opened up their lives in allowing her to care for them and their precious newborns during such a vulnerable time of need. Sarah has a deep connection to Aboriginal health and has worked in senior government roles as an Aboriginal ally, supporting policy

The 50s Compass

implementation and sector development. She holds a Bachelor of Nursing, Graduate Diploma Nursing, Masters in Public Health and most recently a Graduate Certificate in Mental Health.

Sarah loves seeing people, especially women, operating to their full potential. She is committed to supporting them to pursue their dreams while balancing the many aspects of daily life. Through the sharing of stories and providing thought provoking content within her book, Sarah hopes that those who read it will be empowered to navigate their compass and embrace their full potential. The content will encourage deep reflection, inspire action and provide a roadmap for living with purpose, vitality and a sense of fulfilment, no matter where you are in your midlife journey.

Special Thanks

To write a book, especially your first book, it takes a special group of people who believe in what you do, support you and want to see you become a successful author. I never imagined that by starting this journey, I would even be writing this section!

Thanking Myself

First of all, a special shout out to myself! Thanks Self because without you I would never have done this. I spoke to my inner critic and told her to pipe down, I spoke to my inner feminine archetypes the Huntress and the Queen and they both loudly told me to keep going. Thanks gals; because look at me now!

Natasa Denman

Natasa is one of the most dynamic and vivacious entrepreneurial women I have ever encountered. She makes the Road Runner look slow! Her knowledge and expertise in the process of writing a book is incredible. She started her business The Ultimate 48 Hour Author in May 2010 and her proven ability to guide and mentor in writing a first book is something I will never forget. She is living proof that we as women, mothers, wives and thought leaders can achieve anything we want.

https://www.writeabook.com.au/

The Ultimate 48 Hour Author Team and Community

It's not often you encounter a whole team and community that shows genuine commitment and support for each and every individual. That is what I thank the team and community of The Ultimate 48 Hour Author for. They have all created a safe and nurturing environment to learn the tools that have enabled me to become a first time author. Natasa and Stuart with their extended team have provided the foundational knowledge and continuous support to write and build a business around my passion for writing. The extended community of other authors have inspired me to keep going and connect with like-minded individuals who are going to continue to lift me up and move me forward. I say an enormous thank you.

https://48.ultimate48hourauthor.com.au

Special Thanks

My Parents

I take a moment to thank my parents. Without their commitment to bringing me up in a world that spoke to the narrative, 'You can do anything you want as long as you work hard,' I wouldn't have achieved half of my successes thus far. In everything I do, there is the blend of their values and mirroring what they have exemplified in my life. I thank them for their guidance, support, unwavering dedication to any crazy idea that I have and for the wise words of wisdom that accompanies this.

Those Incredible Women and People in my Circle

I literally have no words of thanks that can even begin to touch the sides of the gratitude jar towards these women and people. This heartfelt thanks is for each and every person who has touched my life. This stems from early childhood teachers, those in my professional career, those during my time raising my children, those I have met travelling the world, those I have nursed and those I have met during my surfing and crazy adventures; the list is long. Each of you have touched my soul and made my journey in life just that much better! You have given me inspiration to write this book.

My Close Circle of Girls

This is a special thanks to the close girlfriends who have stood the test of time and still continue to have me in their lives (I say with a cheeky grin). They have showed patience, support and given me real truths on every challenge and dilemma that I throw at them. They have listened to the same problem over and over again and also listened to me not listening to them! They are my rocks and saviours. You know who you are and I love you girls deeply.

My Younger Circle of Girls

This is a specific shout out to all the younger girls who are in my life. There are quite a few of you and many of you contributed to the content within this book. Each and every one of you holds a special place in my heart. I am in awe of your grit, determination and how you hold your feminine energy in this fast-paced, ridiculous world of technology and somewhat masculine driven environments. You are our future and I am confident that this next wave of women such as yourselves is going to shape an even better future for your children. Continue to rule the world you lot!

Words into Actions

The 50s Compass: Finding Your True North in Midlife is just the beginning. If you are ready to turn inspiration into transformation, I offer several ways to continue your journey; each is designed to help you build on the skills that you already have and continue to move forward with clarity, connection and most of all courage.

Facilitated Workshops
Face-to-face or online workshops tailored to midlife women who are seeking a space for deeper reflection, purpose and a connected community. These personal and more intimate gatherings offer the participants a safe space with like-minded individuals for guided inquiry. There are practical exercises, reflective prompts and opportunities for sharing stories that will support you to realign with your True North.

Speaking at Events
Building on my professional experience as a public speaker during my nursing career, with warmth and relatability, I continue to speak to audiences about the power and potential of midlife and beyond. I speak from living experience and address topics such as identity shifts, maintaining health and vitality, exploring spirituality through the lens of feminine and masculine energies and most of all, rediscovering passion in all domains of life. Each talk is tailored to the respective audience to inspire, challenge and uplift with practical take home tools.

Online Membership: The Compass Circle
A supportive online community through a monthly subscription. This offering allows for monthly interactive online workshops, live coaching sessions and reflective tools. It's a space to gather from the comfort of your own home or anywhere that you are around the world. The Compass Circle brings together people who share the same love to grow, learn, connect and be the best version of ourselves.

Speaker Bio

Sarah Ong is a passionate advocate for women navigating the ever-changing landscape of midlife. As a registered nurse with specialist qualifications in Neonatal Intensive Care, Public Health, Mental Health and Project Management, Sarah brings over two decades of experience in mentoring and supporting others through life's personal and professional pivotal moments with compassion and clarity.

As the creator of *The 50s Compass: Finding Your True North in Midlife,* Sarah blends personal insights with professional wisdom to support women in rediscovering purpose, vitality and realignment in their midlife and beyond. Her work is grounded in the belief that this chapter of life is not about slowing down, but a powerful opportunity to reawaken oneself and return to what truly matters.

As a mother of four, Sarah recognises the challenges that many face throughout busy day to day life. Therefore, when she's not writing, speaking or leading workshops, Sarah can be found by

The 50s Compass

the ocean paddling out on her longboard, lifting weights at the gym, or inspiring others through meaningful daily connections and conversations through her own vibrant approach to living fully.

Sarah's offerings include speaking at events, whether that be corporate or local gatherings, workshop facilitation, program guidance and 1:1 mentoring sessions. She offers these services under her Consultancy Company: SJO Consultancy which has been registered since 2021.

P: 0421 640 186 | E: sarahjane1073@gmail.com

Disclaimer

This book is a collection of insights, reflections and personal stories that I've gathered through my own life and from experiences and interactions I've had with others along the way. While I have drawn from real conversations, readings and my professional experiences, *The 50s Compass* is not intended to replace professional medical, psychological, financial or legal advice.

The stories, including those based on real people have been shared with permission or altered to protect privacy. Any resemblance to individuals outside these intended portrayals is purely coincidence.

My hope is that through reading this book you are inspired and encouraged to pursue your own reflections. As always, please seek appropriate support and advice when making decisions and taking actions that impact your health and wellbeing.

Notes

The 50s Compass

Notes

www.ingramcontent.com/pod-product-compliance
Lightning Source LLC
Chambersburg PA
CBHW060454080526
44584CB00015B/1436